A Measure of Failure

A Measure of Failure

The Political Origins
of Standardized Testing

Mark J. Garrison

Published by State University of New York Press, Albany

© 2009 State University of New York

Printed in the United States of America

For information, contact State University of New York Press, Albany, NY
www.sunypress.edu

Production by Ryan Morris
Marketing by Fran Keneston

Library of Congress Cataloging-in-Publication Data

Garrison, Mark J., 1968–
   A measure of failure : the political origins of standardized testing / Mark J.
Garrison.
     p. cm.
   Includes bibliographical references and index.
   ISBN 978-1-4384-2777-5 (hardcover : alk. paper) — ISBN 978-1-4384-2778-2
(pbk. : alk. paper)
   1. Achievement tests—United States—History. 2. Education—Standards—
United States—History. I. Title.
   LB3060.3.G37 2009
   371.26'20973—dc22

2008051366

10 9 8 7 6 5 4 3 2 1

Contents

Preface

For years I have been fascinated with our society's growing reliance on the "social technology" of standardized testing (Madaus 1990) and the so-called standards movement in which it plays a key role. This technology seems to inspire such discontent and controversy, yet it, like prison construction, is one of the country's most consistent growth industries (Haney, Madaus, and Lyons 1993; Pile 2005). The emphasis on such tests seems to grow despite intense and periodic opposition, a cacophony of resistance that now seems to have reached a historic crescendo with the unprecedented testing mandates of the No Child Left Behind Act of 2001 (NCLB).[1]

This interest did not convert easily into a research program, however. For years I struggled simply with how to conceptualize the question, and how to shed new light on what is admittedly a well-worn topic. The scope and sheer volume of this literature is awe-inspiring—and suspect given what I take to be limited advances in the theory, practice, and critical analysis of educational assessment.

The block, I finally came to understand, is the preoccupation with whether standardized tests are "bad" or "good," "fair" or "biased," or measurements of "nature or nurture." After years of engaging in such debates, taking classes on test construction, and reading what both proponents and critics have to say about standardized tests, I realized that we needed to ask different questions, and throw away what amounts to a broken record.

How is it that admittedly intelligent people have such divergent and opposing views of standardized tests, one group claiming for them the mantel of objectivity and fairness, the other disparaging them as crooked yardsticks whose only consistent hallmark is bias (e.g., Sacks 2000)? If standardized tests are so controversial and the objects of both litigation and ridicule, and if they are so suspect in their claims to accuracy and objectivity, why do we increasingly rely on them (McDonnell 2004, 9)? Thus my research began more with a focus on why a society adopts a particular standard during a particular period in time: how and why did standardized tests become the ubiquitous standard by which achievement and intelligence are measured?[2] Why, for example, are standardized tests given as the standard for what it means to be fair, or nonbiased? Without a clear understanding of the origins of this ubiquitous standard, alternatives to it will remain out of reach.

I began to ask this question when I realized that standardized tests have been used to meet seemingly opposing agendas, whether by courts, legislatures, or policy makers (McDonnell 2004; Resnick 1981). The same tools that are used to show schools are "failing" are also said to improve them, though the documentation of failure seems to grossly outpace actual improvement. Sometimes obtaining a low score on a standardized test is required for increased funding, while other times only high scores on these tests result in support or opportunity. Proponents have correctly argued, I think, that tests can function to open up "gates" as much as they can close these "gates" (National Commission on Testing and Public Policy 1990).

But different interpretations of standardized test scores nonetheless assume a reliance on standardized tests of achievement and intelligence. This commonality is significant. It functions to quietly set boundaries on public and policy discourse just as legal statutes set boundaries on court rulings (Dorn 1998). This book is premised in part on the assumption that we need to remove the existing boundaries to discussions about educational standards.

So, for example, why do we have "gates" and why do we watch over them with "mental tests"? How and why did mental tests and academic standards come to be considered central to the project of organizing a democratic society? What is the significance of the role of standardized tests in the theme that American schools are failing? What impact will the demise of public education have, given its historically central role in American political thought (Welter 1962)?

Answering these questions will assist in developing a better analysis of the so-called standards or accountability movement and also, hopefully, give rise to a broader consciousness of what is at stake in the present reform environment and the extensive social transformation required to develop alternatives. Without a clear understanding of why the United States adopted standardized tests as the ubiquitous standard for education, efforts to improve education with alternative measures will meet with mixed results at best (McDonnell 2004; Smith 1996; Smith, Heinecke, and Noble 1999).

Why Another Book on Testing?

Despite more than a century of sometimes intense criticism, standardized tests are now being presented as a linchpin in the latest education reform agenda, the key mechanism to holding teachers, students, schools—even parents—accountable to new, ostensibly high academic goals (I cannot help but laugh at those who present the nineteenth-century standard of basic literacy for all as some noble and lofty goal). And while many educators have expressed the view that the standards movement is just another fad, state and federal agencies continue to increase their reliance on standardized tests. Relative to other education programs, the use of standardized tests to reform education has had a long gestation period with sustained growth, now seemingly in a period of maturation (Linn 2000).

While it may seem to some fairly easy to render standardized tests as pseudoscience, harmful, and so on, alternatives appear to be both unworkable and at odds with basic cultural assumptions. Put another way, debunking the tests—without analyzing them in their sociohistorical context—appears to have done little good, and in some ways now contributes to the crisis faced by public education. Few seem to realize, for example, that rejecting standardized tests in the American context might actually mean rejecting the notion of equal opportunity as a basis for structuring education. For without an alternative theory and practice of assessment *and a political order that will support it*, the rejection of standardized tests morphs into a rejection of standards altogether. I regularly point out to my students the irrationality of their proposition that educators oppose standards, asking if they object to the question, Are you for or against having an economy? Of course, the point is what kind of economy, or what standard, whose interest does it serve, and so on.

Thus a clearer understanding of the nature and origin of standardized tests is needed. It is no longer enough to link their history to the eugenics movement and various forms of structural inequality (e.g., Kamin 1974; Mensh and Mensh 1991); it is no longer enough to document the means by which test-based accountability exacerbates inequality (e.g., McNeil 2000). It is no longer enough to depict standards as yet another form of the free-market's "disciplinary power" (Mathison and Ross 2002). While very important contributions to the analysis and critique of standardized testing exist, I think we need to move beyond what typically amounts to discrediting. There are, I think, unexplored presuppositions of standardized testing that up to this point have blocked us from achieving the common goal of affirming an education for all, that affirms all.

While I admittedly believe that the present standards reform effort is a destructive one, I also see dangerous misconceptions in criticisms of testing: the pervasive belief that standardization is necessarily harmful to students and teachers, that merit should be the object of educational assessment, or that equity (or fairness) is an appropriate criteria when determining what students have learned. With my focus on politics, I also hope to assist previous efforts in distinguishing more clearly what issues related to assessment are psychological in nature and what issues are political in nature. It will be a very important contribution, I think, if more headway can be made in these areas.

Finally, while most commentators debate the degree to which testing contributes to building a social order based on merit, few ask why standardized tests became the standard for educational merit when numerous other possibilities existed. That tests are used by those pushing for privatization only begs, once again, this question, Why are standardized tests playing such a key role in debates about the future of public education?

Acknowledgments

While it seems customary to thank one's family and friends last, I wish to break with that tradition. Without the support of my wife, Melissa, and two children, Linnea and Casimir—all who queried why it took me so long to produce such a modest book—I would not have been able to complete the task. I dedicate this book to them, not simply as my way of thanking them for their support, but also because they, like families everywhere, are bearing the brunt of the offensive against public education and are eager for a way out of the crisis. I hope that my efforts contribute.

I also appreciate the patience and support of my friends who have dedicated themselves to political organizing and the renewal of the society. They have provided me with insights I could not obtain from books while at the same time stressing the importance of completing one.

As I sat down to write this acknowledgments section, I became overwhelmed at just how many people have assisted me throughout the years. Foremost is my friend and colleague Shawgi Tell. He is noted for his encouragement, including organizing my first professional speaking opportunity on this topic; but he also stands out for being the only person to insist that he be acknowledged! A special thanks goes to my close friend and public school English teacher, Pete Lund, for making notable efforts at improving the readability of a text written by someone who is a much better orator than a writer of academic prose.

As this book is derived from my dissertation, a special thanks to my dissertation chair, Hank Bromley, and committee member, S. G. Grant, are in order. For giving feedback on early drafts of sections of the book, and the offerings he makes available on his blog, I thank Sherman Dorn. Many of my colleagues in the New York State Foundations of Education Association also deserve thanks as they provided the opportunity for young scholars such as myself to test out their analyses in a friendly yet intellectually challenging atmosphere. Here, a special thanks to Norm Bauer is in order. Raymond Horn's support of my work resulted in publications of earlier drafts of parts of this volume and that recognition played an important role in encouraging me to complete the project. Serge Nicolas was especially helpful in providing me with key manuscripts regarding the history of the work of Alfred

Binet. And my work in France would have been impossible and certainly less enjoyable without the support and efforts of Ali Ait Si Mhamed, who translated both texts and conversations while in Paris and after. I would also like to thank Sue Books, Richard Gibson, Sandra Mathison, and Richard Quantz for their thoughtful and supportive correspondence.

Special thanks is also extended to Greenwood Press for granting me permission to use portions of my chapter "What Are We Measuring? A Reexamination of Psychometric Practice and the Problem of Assessment in Education," in *The Praeger Handbook of Education and Psychology*, 4 vols., ed. Joe L. Kincheloe and Raymond A. Horn, 814–823 (Westport, CT: Praeger, 2006), which appear in chapters 3 and 4. Special thanks also to Caddo Gap Press for granting me permission to us portions of my article "Measure, Mismeasure, or Not Measurement at All? Psychometrics as Political Theory" in *Practitioner Quarterly: A Journal for the Scholar-Practitioner Leader* 2 (4) (2004): 61–76, which appear in chapters 3 and 4..

The reviewers for State University of New York (SUNY) Press were immensely useful in preparing the final manuscript; I appreciate the time and care they took in providing critical feedback. In particular, a special thanks to Kenneth Saltman. Having blown his cover as an anonymous reviewer in the narrative sent to me by SUNY Press, I can thank him for his suggestions. Even those I have chosen to forgo were beneficial as they helped me argue out more clearly the significance of my findings, and saved me from some embarrassment. A special thanks to Lisa Chesnel who assisted me at SUNY Press is also warranted, as she never tired, remaining supportive and enthusiastic. My research assistant, Joanne Hernick, also deserves a great deal of credit for her assistance in finalizing the manuscript and promises to stand out as the book's biggest advocate!

Finally, I would like to thank my colleagues at D'Youville College for their encouragement, financial support, and release time from teaching duties. Without their support, completion of the text would have been unattainable. My students remain an important inspiration and anyone who has taught knows that students have a way of indicating to an emerging author a gem appearing in an otherwise half-baked and poorly constructed lecture. It is to them that I will continue to look for continued inspiration for future work.

1

A Measure of Failure

The idea underlying the implementation of written examinations [in the nineteenth century], that they could provide information about student learning, was born in the minds of individuals already convinced that education was substandard in quality. This sequence—perception of failure followed by the collection of data designed to document failure . . . offers early evidence of what has become a tradition of school reform and a truism of student testing: tests are often administered not just to discover how well schools or kids are doing, but rather to obtain external *confirmation*—validation—of the hypothesis that they are not doing well at all. (Office of Technology Assessment 1992, 108)

I had marked "Nota Bene" on this passage more than ten years ago as a graduate student. It struck me as a very important yet underexplored observation. Why this evident preoccupation with the failure of public education? I became particularly interested in the significance of the present trend to use the results of standardized tests to justify the elimination of public education "as we know it" when I began to understand that this technology originated to justify and help erect our public education system.[1]

This observation led me to carry out the case studies of Horace Mann and Alfred Binet that are the mainstay of this book. In each, the documentation of failure—the failure of the then existing Boston public schools, the extensive "retardation" existing in French schools and their failure to properly identify and educate "mental defectives"—facilitated reforms of those time periods. Advances in testing accompanied the documentation of failure, where mental tests were said to not only identify but also remedy the situation. Thus, standardized tests originated in a crucible of failure. In each case, the reader will see that standardized tests of either achievement or ability were tools used to institute and justify substantive changes in the governance and functioning of education.

This book argues that standardized testing technology originated as a tool of liberal (or representative) democracy that enables the system to present as egalitarian a social order that values social difference. In this context, the once unimportant idea of mental ability became a basis for political rights (Carson 1994). As public schools developed, they increasingly assumed the role of marking such abilities. Academic tests emerged to serve this purpose constituting an ideological tool for justifying social inequality (fair competition), a political tool for securing state power and affirming the power of public office and the professions (accountability), and a philosophical tool for justifying public governance of education and for educating "the masses" or public (reason or judgment).

The case studies show that tests of achievement and ability emerged to mark the then existing educational institutions as failures, for these existing arrangements could not meet the needs of the then emerging social orders. The new tests served as instantiations of the new model and purpose of education established by a new authority or governing arrangement. An emphasis on testing is, this research suggests, an outgrowth of a crisis evident in an intensifying political fight between factions of elite, on the one hand, and between social classes, on the other. This book exists to argue out the aforementioned to provide background to the present testing movement. It should make clear that neither in the past nor the present is testing mainly about "improving education." It is, instead, about control over the purpose and nature of schooling.

Failure and Crisis

The emphasis on failure in reports about public education is as significant as it is problematic. Debates about public school failure tend to give a great deal of emphasis to interpreting standardized test data, with the future of public education purportedly hinged to these data, especially when discussed within the framework of the No Child Left Behind Act (NCLB) and its mandate that public schools come under the discipline of the federally subsidized "free market" when Adequate Yearly Progress is not reached (e.g., mandates for charters, and the for-profit provisions of tutoring services). Methodological questions as they relate to conclusions about the efficacy of a particular program or public education as a whole have long dominated the academic discussion (e.g., Berliner 1993; Bracey 2002; Saltman 2005; Stedman 1996). But lacking in these debates is an understanding of the conceptions of failure and of crisis and the significance of such designations.

Foremost is the need to acknowledge that failure points to the problem of reproduction: the claim that an institution is failing is a claim that it cannot reproduce or serve its social function. It is the claim that something cannot be repaired, but must instead be replaced. But failure is also a designation of value. To designate something as a failure is to devalue it; the discourse of failure serves to discredit. Failure, too, is real—even propaganda about failure has to have a real basis. The fact is, public schools have failed to meet the educational needs of large sections of the people— what is unique in the present is that public schools appear to be unable to play their social reproduction function as in the past. The accountability movement and the central role standardized tests play within that movement is in part an outgrowth of this reality (see Dorn 2007).

Generally speaking, failure means "omitting to perform something due or required," a notion that implies a standard, an expectation of performance, especially when performance is understood as role or responsibility. Importantly, the Oxford English Dictionary (OED) gives another sense of failure as "becoming exhausted or running short, breaking down in health, declining in strength or activity." Thus failure can signify breakdowns in social relations or institutions, which may be "breaking down in health, declining in strength," so to speak.[2]

Originating in the seventeenth century, the word *failure* referenced a breach in justice and the problem of succession (bloodlines). Immediately, then, one sees its original connection to politics. Justice, a notion connected to legal systems and the state, is required for the legitimacy and thus longevity of a political order. Outlining the development of the conception of failure, the OED gives this example from Mountstuart Elphinstone's 1815 *An Account of the Kingdom of Caubul*: "On the failure of issue . . . an adopted son succeeds." This suggests in particular that failure references a breakdown in the reproduction of political systems. Reformers such as Mann and Binet, the reader will see, sought to resolve social contradictions by giving a greater role to government-controlled schools in reproducing the social order. Standardized exams were developed as markers of failure, and stood as justifications for and symbols of the changes reformers sought.

A time period marked by failure is a turning point, where what has been is dying away, no longer sustainable by any social force, and what is coming into being has yet to take hold, with no force clearly in control. These turning points are by definition periods of crisis, and I take the two case studies in this book to be periods of crisis. The word *crisis*, according to the OED, comes from the Greek meaning to separate, to decide; crisis is given as the point in time "when it is decided whether an affair or course of action shall proceed, be modified, or terminated," or more generally an "unstable state of affairs in which a decisive change is impending."

Thus, instead of assuming a "manufactured" crisis—a position all too common in my view, one that tends to presume that society develops according to the wishes of those in elite positions—I take assertions of crisis seriously. It has been said that such proclamations are mere hyperbole, the rhetoric of clever politicians with a hidden agenda. This is, of course, partly true and generally well documented (Bracey 2002; Saltman 2005). But this is limited in terms of analysis.

Rendering the crisis in education and society as a fabrication of the elite veils why the elite (the bankers, industrialists, and key politicians) would work so hard to destroy that which those in their position one hundred fifty years ago worked so hard to build as necessary for maintaining their political system and their power? On what basis is this institution—public education—no longer serving its functions, from their point of view? Why use tests to discredit this institution when they proved so useful in establishing it? And what significance and opening does this crisis have for defending rights and for people's genuine empowerment and public participation?

A final word is in order regarding the role of standards in discussions of failure and crisis. The issue is not so much to debate whether schools are failing, for this is, in fact, an abstraction. "Failure to perform a duty or action" is a specific thing, that is, it refers to failure to perform something. The thesis is that the standards used to judge the success of schools have changed, and that this change in standards is about shifts in power and purpose, not "school improvement." What schools are expected to do by those officials who now wield power is different from the past, and this difference is reflected in their adoption of different standards than those put into place by their predecessors. That business leaders were, for example, directed by the Business Roundtable to sit on "cut score committees" to ensure high levels of failure is a remarkable example of the role of standards in establishing power (Business Roundtable 1998) and more generally of standardized testing as a measure of failure.

Chapter Overview

Oriented by historical sociology, chapter 2 presents a heuristic for analyzing standards based in a review of literature tracing the nature and function of standards of both physical (e.g., length) and extraphysical (e.g., academic achievement) phenomena. Standards are explored as weapons in the quest for power, as a means to give material expression to a philosophy or aim, and as embodiments of the social values of a culture or class. The heuristic poses four interrelated themes to guide the analysis. Chapter 3 explores the notions of achievement and ability as forms of vertical classification, where notions of ability and achievement are explored as basic tenets of

Anglo-American political thought, that natural distinctions should be the basis for ordering society. Chapter 4 argues that standardized tests—as concrete expressions of the cultural meaning of achievement and ability—function to assess social value. Social value is the idea that human beings exist in distinct hierarchical groupings in terms of their value or worth. It also refers to the process by which individual or group value is socially attached to a position within a hierarchically structured social system. Standardized testing—or the theory and practice known as "psychometrics"—the fourth chapter argues, is not a form of measurement. Psychometrics is best understood as the development of tools for vertical classification and the production of social value.

Chapter 5 presents and examines the political origin of standardized testing in the emergence of nation states and political arrangements favoring capital as a class (against feudal political arrangements) and the role their new theory of governance gave to reason and the so-called natural aristocracy. As it is well suited to "develop new theories capable of providing more convincing and comprehensive explanations for historical patterns and structures" by focusing in on the growth of national states (Bonnell 1980, 161; see also Green 1990; Tilly 1981), the approach of historical sociology is adopted. The role given to formal education in nation building is explored as an important condition for the emergence of standardized tests of achievement and ability and the linkage of mental ability to rights, especially the right to govern and the role given to enlightened public opinion in governance.

Adopting Bonnell's (1980) method of case-illustration, whereby different cases are compared to a single theory or concept, two key points or cases in the development of standardized testing in education are analyzed. The first case, involving Horace Mann, is explored in chapter 6. It examines the Boston Grammar School Committee's efforts to develop what is considered the first large-scale use of standardized test methods to "secure positive, objective information about the products of classroom instruction" (Caldwell and Courtis 1925; Resnick 1982). While for hundreds of years various oral examinations and school visitations had been used to assess educational progress and select and certify pupils, this development marks the beginning of achievement testing as we know it today. Mann's use of these tests helped bring the Boston public schools under state supervision, establish practices consistent with notions of equal opportunity in education while also supporting the common school reform agenda, including everything from the age-graded classroom to state-run teachers colleges.

After decades of unfruitful work to measure mental capacities of various kinds, and wide variation in the definition and classification of intelligence, chapter 7 explores the work of Alfred Binet and his colleagues to develop the first practical means to measure "intelligence." Since that time, this "IQ" test has become the standard by which intelligence in children and adults is measured and defined (Sarason 1976). Binet's work took place in the context of the secularization of the French school system. It helped establish common standards for the identification of students who would not benefit from "normal instruction." This work was instrumental in institutionalizing "tracking" and a new model of "equal opportunity" where different groups of students were to receive different forms of education based on their future roles in society (Coleman 1977). Binet's test was guided by a desire to "engineer" society and avoid social unrest. These historical points in the development of standardized tests are examined in chapter 8 using the previously outlined heuristic. In particular, they enable us to explore the ways in which standardized tests of achievement and ability functioned to institutionalize notions about the role of merit in establishing a legitimate political order, and the role of public education in informing that merit and validating its public expression. Both cases reveal standardized tests as mechanisms for the assessment of social value, a practice embedded in a larger political project that rewrote the rights and responsibilities of both government and citizen. The book concludes with a summary of the case studies in light of the analysis and heuristic outlined. Implications for these findings for the present context are suggested.

2

The Nature and
Function of Standards

The perspective of historical sociology suggests that standards be examined as they relate to the history of political patterns and structures (Bonnell 1980; Green 1990; Tilly 1981). While selection, certification, system monitoring, and improvement are often given as the functions of assessment in education (Broadfoot 1996), and thus the starting points for analysis, I present and argue for an alternative heuristic, one that focuses on the standard as such. This perspective emphasizes a standard's role in establishing and maintaining an authority, its interests, and outlook, a perspective synthesized from Kula's (1986) historical study of physical measures and consistent with historical treatments of competitive academic exams in Britain, France, and China (e.g., Carson 1994; Menzel 1963; Roach 1971).

Definitions

The central concept for this analysis is that of standard. The etymology of the word suggests a flag, or flag to mark a rallying place. Probably of Germanic origin, the first part of this word is derived from *stantan*, to stand; the second element comes from *ort*, a point or corner. As a noun it has several related definitions, according to Webster's Dictionary. For example, it is given as "a pole or spear bearing some conspicuous object (as a banner) at the top formally used in an army or fleet to mark a rallying point, to signal, or to serve as an emblem." It is something that is "established by authority, custom, or general consent as a model or example to be followed." Importantly "criterion" and "test" are given as synonyms for "standard." And finally a standard is "something that is set up and established by authority as a rule for the measure of quantity, weight, extent, value, or quality." As an adjective, Webster's offers the definitions of

7

"constituting or affording a standard for comparison, measurement, or judgment" as in standard weight, and "having qualities or attributes required by law or established by custom."[1]

Standards and Political Power

A major precept for this work is that setting standards is a function of political authority, bound up with the political theory and social values of that authority. This precept is derived from Witold Kula's (1986) study, *Measures and Men*, and is supported by historical analyses of examinations in Britain, France, and China.

On the basis of examining the relationship between the development of standards of physical properties (such as length and weight) and a society's political arrangements, Kula observed:

> The right to determine measures is an attribute of authority in all advanced societies. It is the prerogative of the ruler to make measures mandatory and to retain the custody of the standards[. . . .] The controlling authority, moreover, seeks to unify all measures within its territory and claim the right to punish metrological transgressions. (1986, 18)

He further notes that the "frequent struggles centered about metrological competence of the constituted power are but a manifestation of the rivalry between various organs of authority aspiring to control measures in order to bolster their standing," emphasizing that "attempts to control measures [standards] have been an ever-present element in the struggle for power between interested representatives of the privileged class" (18–19). Measures become one means by which conflicting claims are sorted out. The failure of established measures to sort out confiscating claims might signal the failure of the authority they represent.

While Kula offers numerous examples throughout his book to support such a generalization, possibly the clearest come from France. Kula traces the thousand-years history of mostly failed attempts to standardize measures that preceded the French Revolution. After presenting various normative declarations of Charlemagne and his successors, Kula writes:

> The Crown's program in metrological matters . . . was not to change in a thousand years. It rests upon the recognition of the royal prerogative in the field of weights and measures as an attribute of royal sovereignty. The standard kept in the palace would hold sway over the entire area where the royal writ ran; the

standardizing plans therefore applied to the state's entire territory. At the same time we have here some reliable evidence, bearing witness as early as the Carolingian period to the duality of metrological practice that, too, was to last a thousand years: namely, different measures for buying and for selling, for collecting and for distributing, and, also, the increasing of measures employed in collecting taxes in kind. (1986, 162)

Albeit with modest success, the French monarch repeatedly intervened in metrological matters in order to restrict the sovereignty claims of the seigneurs (or lords) and to enforce royal institutions throughout the kingdom, thus advancing the cause of unification (167). Such unification would wait, however, until the "rational unity in its social and spatial dimensions" took hold "at the expense of the privileged class." Declaration by the third estate that "it is representative of the nation," was a prelude to the bourgeois, antifeudal revolution. This radical social transformation was marked by the call: "One King, One Law, One Weight, One Measure" (see chap. 22)

While Kula focuses attention on measures of the physical (such as length or mass), some historical investigations of academic standards in the form of examinations or tests suggest that these social technologies have long been associated with the establishment and maintenance of political power (Madaus 1990). According to British historians, there is an important link between the increase in academic competition at the universities and of academically qualified politicians during the nineteenth century (Montgomery 1967, 1978; Roach 1971). Mathews asserts that the impact of competitive examinations on access to positions of political and professional authority were on a historical scale quite rapid. He notes however that "it is doubtful whether those in business and industry owed much to examinations despite the extraordinary growth of the public schools and the numbers of the sons of the middle classes who attended them" (1985, 8). Arguing out the political utility of competitive written exams, England's leading nineteenth-century politician W. E. Gladstone wrote the following to Queen Victoria: "I do not hesitate to say that one of the great recommendations of the change (to open competition) in my eyes would be its tendency to strengthen and multiply the ties between the higher classes and the possession of administrative power. . . . I have a strong impression that the aristocracy of this country are even superior in natural gifts, on the average, to the mass," he said, "but it is plain that with their acquired advantages their insensible education [sic], irrespective of book learning, they have an immense superiority. This applies in its degrees to all those who may be called gentlemen by birth and training" (Hanson 1993, 199).

France offers yet another clear example of the link between academic standards and the establishment and maintenance of political power. The meritocratic educational structures created following the French Revolution are possibly some of the clearest examples of the link between competitive academic examinations and political systems in the modern period. These competitive exams served not only to centralize power, "but to identify, or create, talent within the French citizenry and to enlist it in the service of the state" (Carson 1994, 99). The relative role of meritocratic arrangements in creating a new elite as opposed to democratizing the French educational system was a constant theme during this time period (Carson 1994, 104).

Yet the classic example of the connection between academic standards and political power comes from China. Max Weber speculated that Chinese civil service exams were linked to efforts to maintain a dynasty's supreme authority. Indeed, other scholars have shown how the treatment of regional quotas in the examination system was used by a dynasty to achieve political ends.

> The first significant increase [in the use of competitive examinations] came abruptly with the rise to power of the ambitious empress Wu Tse-t'ien. Her sharp eye discerned in the technique of examination, it seems, a tool for her projected usurpation of power. It might serve to tap the heretofore neglected source of trained men in the Southeast and help to dislodge from power the tightly knit clique from the capital region, which was devoted to the interests of the reigning dynasty. (Kracke 1963, 69)

Over time, as with France and England, the examination system came to occupy a central place in Chinese political theory, as a legitimate basis for sorting out contests over who would hold what power. And certainly the following Confucian aphorism speaks to the role of competitive exams in justifying political power: "When the right men are available, government flourishes. When the right men are not available, government declines" (Menzel 1963, x).

With this last example we are directed to explore academic examinations, not only as they are connected with establishing or breaking political loyalties, but also as they are connected with legitimating a political order or policy. The British sociologist Eggleston argues that standardized exams do not function mainly to determine social position. "This is not to say that the examination does not play an important, even inescapable role in reproduction," he explains, "but rather that this role is essentially a legitimating and not a determining role" (1986, 61). Historians have, in fact, noted how early twentieth-century school administrators often defended their decisions on the basis of standardized test data (Resnick 1981, 625). In one of the earliest and most thorough studies of the policy impact of standardized testing, Kellaghan and his colleagues found that "testing was used to support an already-established policy decision rather than to determine a policy, with test results playing a complementary or confirmatory role" (Kellaghan, Madaus, and Airasian 1982, 246; see also Airasian 1988). Such findings are, in fact, consistent with the entire history of testing in the United States (Office of Technology Assessment 1992, 108). Legitimacy is a political not an academic function, since it is connected to decision making. Standardized testing is understood by the culture as the appropriate means by which to justify decisions, whether they be about individuals or school systems.

Standards and Social Philosophy

Practices "bound up with man's attitude to measurement," notes Kula, "assume the character of a symbolic expression of many elements of popular 'social philosophy,'" or what is socially desirable, significant, and by extension, what is socially undesirable, insignificant (1986, 9). Examples given are numerous and wide-ranging, from the theological significance of "just measures" in Muslim and Judeo-Christian texts to the folk wisdom of peasants regarding measures of vodka at the local tavern. In this light it becomes quite significant that justifications for standardized tests are predicated on notions of "equal opportunity" and "meritocracy," basic tenets of Anglo-American social and political thought.

    It appears that assessment—the use of standards in the judgment of value—is a feature of the earliest forms of stratified human society. Sociologists point out that there have always been arrangements for formally recognizing the capacity to perform important social roles and to exercise their associated social status and power (Eggleston 1986, 59). Notice that there are, in fact, two capacities referenced here. The first is the capacity to perform the role itself (functional competency), and the second capacity is to exercise the role's associated social status and power (what might be called "social competency"). Notions of ability, of capacity, are bound up with social roles, for ability must have a place for it to be manifest. This quality or state of being able manifests itself in the "physical, mental, or legal power to perform," according to Webster's. Note that ability can signify a power inhering in persons—again functional capacity—or a legal power to do something, or social capacity. It is significant, I think, that the etymology of ability is from the Middle English, suitability. In this regard, standardized test-based assessment is the judgment of worth relative to a structural slot or social position—what is deemed of value and who is deemed of value—a process abstracted as achievement or ability. It also appears that achievement tests produce abstracted values of institutions or components thereof while ability tests produce abstracted values of individuals, each process, of course, having implications for the other. It will be important to keep this in mind for the time periods when each form of assessment is developed and emphasized.

It is this second ability that is the object of assessment via standardized tests in education, a conjecture that is supported by the relatively strong correlation of test scores with measures of social inequality (what sociology euphemistically labels "socioeconomic status"; or SES) compared to the relatively weak correlation of ability and achievement tests with measures of performance outside academe (Handel 2003; National Commission on Testing and Public Policy 1990).[2]

Ranking human worth on the basis of how well one competes in academic contests, with the effect that high ranks are associated with privilege, status, and power, suggests that psychometry is premised, not on knowledge of intellectual or emotional development, but on Anglo-American political ideals of rule by the best (most virtuous) and the brightest (most talented), a "natural aristocracy" in Jeffersonian parlance. Marking virtue gives rise to status duality, marking talent gives rise to spatial duality; the linkage to social structure is the argument of social value. Western political thought since the seventeenth century postulates talent as concomitant to virtue, and its signifier.

Although more will be said about this in the next three chapters, it is important to note that within the theory of a natural aristocracy (or what is commonly called "meritocracy") there is the assumption that talent signifies virtue, and that virtue qualifies someone for decision-making positions. In other words, meritocracy is a particular type of vertical classification that is centered on competition as a basis for ranking and thus status and power. As with the early Chinese examinations, while character was the preferred object of examination, *ability was substituted as the measure of man* (Menzel 1963). Within the Enlightenment tradition of the West, academic ability is also viewed as a marker of virtue. As just one example, southern Europeans were once barred from immigrating to the United States, justified on the basis of their low IQ scores. The argument of the psychologists was that those who lack intellectual capacity inevitably gravitate toward immoral and criminal behavior. A high score on an IQ test, however, suggests a student is worthy of being trained to play social roles with high status and power—the high score suggests the high status, worth, or virtue (see Chapman 1988). School exams focus on abstruse academic exercises, I think, because they endeavor to assess the ability to exercise a role's attending social status and power—for example, is he or she capable of "good judgment"—and not so much the functional capacities demanded by the role. That is, official educational assessments seem primarily concerned with the second capacity I identified earlier, a capacity that does not inhere in an individual, but rather refers to the fit between the individual and the position. Because the role of truck driver currently has little associated status or power, licensure procedures need only focus on the functional ability itself.

Exercising status and power demands a particular set of aims and values, or else the stability of that status and power is threatened (it is maintenance of the interests of that status and power that seems to be the referent of "good judgment"). Abstruse academic exercises do enforce values, and reflect a definite world outlook or social philosophy. For example, within Euro-American thought, written competitive exams reveal a person's ability to delay gratification, or "self-denial." Roach argues that reformers in England

> put considerable stress on the moral argument at both the individual and the national level. For the individual, examinations are a test of common-sense and of character as well as of book-learning. To do well in them demands perseverance and self-denial which strengthen the character. For the nation, a competitive system would be based on high moral principle and would help to reduce corruption and place seeking. (1971, 30)

That is, the quality that is reflected in doing well on tests of common sense and book learning is good character, a quality that is needed to help establish legitimate government. In this way, it is character that is the object of the examinations.

By the middle of the nineteenth century, on both sides of the Atlantic, written competitive exams pointed to these general abilities, more toward *reasoning* and less on the memorization of facts. In the British context, this ability reflected the gentlemanly values of *quick wit* as well as the ability to reason or judge well. The Cambridge Tripos, a test in logic and reason, rewarded speed and accuracy, just as these qualities insured success in the courtroom (Roach 1971, 13–14).

Another way in which standards reflect social values is through the level of precision of a given standard. Precision signifies the value of the object of measurement. The more advanced the standard, the more that thing or phenomenon is valued. Kula observes that "in societies where land was relatively abundant, the system of area measures tended to be poorly developed" (1986, 6), and the contrary in societies where land was scarce. The same tendency is observed with measures of weight. With the Ashanti of Ghana, one finds a very advanced system of weights, "in whose economy the extraction of gold dust played a major part" (6). Speaking specifically about the question of value, Kula argues that "the more valuable the object, the finer the measure [standard] employed in its measurement." He continues noting that determinations of measuring procedures are partly practical, but cautions that "practical considerations afford only a partial explanation. . . . Our emotive, 'feeling' attitude to the object centers upon its 'value' for man" (88).

This general proposition can be seen at work with social value if we take the example of driving a truck versus becoming a physician. Driving a truck can be said, on this basis, not to be of great social value, for the standard to obtain such a license is not very fine, or precise, even though the safety of millions of travelers and billions of dollars worth of products are at stake. One either passes or fails the relevant tests. Unlike with SAT and ACT test results, or more to the point, elaborate rankings of college and university programs, there is no elaborate hierarchy of licenses. Academic achievement and ability, the standards for entering medical school, are thus highly valued, reflected on the fineness of their measure despite the lack of empirical evidence for such claims to precision (see Gentile 1997). The great effort toward precision is not based on measurement, but instead constitutes a means by which to identify and produce value. That there is a great deal of fineness in the standard of the second and not in the first suggests which is held in greater esteem by the dominant culture. We might expect this situation to change radically if truck drivers somehow got themselves involved in policy making. That is, those who are deemed to occupy sacred positions (good character, high ability) are fit to make decisions, to decide important questions of who, what, where and when.

Standards Reflect Aims

The original meaning of a standard "as formerly used in an army or fleet to mark a rallying point, to signal, or to serve as an emblem" suggests that standards are instances of aims, of ideologies and philosophies. So, for example, the location of the army's flag (standard) signifies just how far the army has advanced relative to its overall political objective. The symbol that stands for an army also becomes a measure of its success.

Webster's Dictionary presents the following: Standard, criterion, test, yardstick, touchstone "can designate, in common, any measure by which one judges a thing as authentic, good, or adequate or the degree to which it is authentic, good, or adequate." Standard "applies to any authoritative rule, principle, or measure used to determine the quantity, weight" or especially "the value, quality, level, or degree of a thing." If a standard is used to judge the value of a person or thing, it follows that it also must have, or be an instance of, that value.

Smallwood's study of grading and examination systems in early American colleges is a useful case in point. The relationship between examinations, grading systems, and standards is best understood, according to her, as follows:

> Because it is much easier to appreciate the concrete than the abstract, standards as conceived by college faculties can best be studied chiefly in terms of entrance requirements and degree regulations. Standards originated in the growth of evaluation methods. Legislation on examinations, grades, entrance, degrees, and special honors naturally resulted from the attempt to establish standards. (1935, 2)

In this example, the demand for standards arises from the need to make some judgment or to be more specific, to evaluate. Rendering the value of something requires a standard be developed. The "attempt to establish standards" was "legislated," or decreed by some authority. Even with the earliest colleges in the United States, evaluations were used to see what progress students, and the institutions they attended, were making *toward the aims* of colleges themselves.

> The supposition has been that the success of a college in accomplishing its aims could be indicated by evaluating the intellectual ability and attainments of its students in the fields of learning offered. The *aims* of a college are the expression of its *philosophy*, and from the very beginnings of education a receptive group of people, called students or scholars, have believed in the philosophy and have *accepted examinations as a measure of their own approach in its realization.* (Smallwood 1935, 2; emphasis added)

With this understanding, standards concretely embody the aims, and therefore stand as a measure of their realization, and, in fact, point to their realization. It is on this basis that exams function both to direct and to motivate.[3]

The relation of the standard as flag or model to the standard as tool in measurement, assessment, and comparison can be explored by briefly examining the problem of "teaching to the test." Teaching to the test, on the one hand, seems consistent with the very nature of a standard, for a test presents "a model or example to be followed." Certainly teachers follow some model. Could arguing against teaching to the test in general be arguing against having a standard, which also may be an argument against having an aim or a philosophy? Is it possible to have an aim without a standard, without some means of judging success?

Yet, the problem critics identify with teaching to the test is not having a model per se. Rather, the problem is that the model (or standard) should assist in reaching some larger goal, and not become the goal itself (as is the case when the goal of teaching is given as raising test scores). In this regard, teaching to the test is the elimination of an aim, and actually goes against the nature of a standard by dislodging it from its raison d'être. Thus, teaching to the test is predicated on the theory that standards are aims, as opposed to the view presented here, which is that standards embody aims, existing to serve something beyond themselves.[4] Struggles over standards and standardized tests in particular are likely rooted in struggles over the aim—the purpose and function of education (Bracey 2002, chap. 2; Ebel 1972, 29–37; Noddings 1997).

Are Standardized Tests Representational or Conventional Measures?

The emergence of metrological concepts and habits is a very important aspect of human apprehension of the world, and of the formation of taxonomic systems and abstract concepts (Kula 1986, 24). This observation is based on the study of physical measures (e.g., length, distance, and weight). One aim of this book as a whole is to establish more fully the utility of applying these precepts to the study of educational standards by exploring the context in which early tests of achievement and intelligence developed.

Yet, the relevance of Kula's study does not simply rest on whether observations of physical measures can be applied to standards for the nonphysical, such as measures of intelligence or academic achievement. Kula's work focuses mainly on the social significance of standards up to the nineteenth century. He delineates two periods in human history, one where standards carry with them a great deal of human significance—representational measures—and the other where the social significance of that standard lies in its lack of symbolic value. These are the abstract and universal measures that came into being with the advent of the metric system. Early measures, Kula writes, "roughly until the beginnings of capitalism, partook of substantive character, 'signified' or represented something, expressed something human relating to man's personality or the condition of his existence." But modern measures, he continues, "have no meaning other than that of sheer convention; what matters is the acceptance of the system, and not the magnitude of the basic unit, which might equally be large or small." Knowledge of physics or astronomy—"the weight of a certain volume of water at a specified temperature and pressure, or a stated part of the meridian"— may be used to establish standards for weights and measures, but "have no social significance" in and of themselves (1986, 120).

Kula identifies precapitalist measures as "anthropomorphic," with the human body and human action as the source of standards. Length might be determined by the forearm or how far one can walk in a day; in advanced, class societies, standards were derived from forearm or stride of the ruler. The standard was human centered, and control over a standard signified power. Adherence to a standard was often used to determine allegiance to the power that established the standard. Standards in production were human centered; cloth, for example, was measured by the forearm of those who worked the loom. Thus with the rise of capitalism, there is a move from "man as the measure of all things" to measures "for all people, for all time," that is, to standards that are established on the basis of abstract and universal qualities or principles.

But in which category should a norm-referenced test be placed? Certainly it appeals to universalism with the statistical abstraction of the normal curve; yet the "norm" is derived from a definite collection of fellow human beings at a definite point in time (anthropomorphic). It can never claim the stability or universal character embodied in the metric system. The social significance of determining the validity of standardized tests on the basis of whether its results correlate with the prevailing inequalities must also be recognized as socially significant. Exploring Kula's analysis of the social significance of the development of abstract standards will help sort this out. Even though they are of the modern industrial era, it should not be taken for granted that standardized norm-referenced tests have progressed in kind with industry and the metric system.

Of the transition from measures rich in their representational quality, with their human associations, "to abstract measures of convention, 'signifying' nothing," Kula writes, points to how "difficult, though, it is to find immutable elements in a world in which nothing stays unchanging! The picture of attempts to find such elements, such fixed points of reference, is therefore full of social values" (1986, 120).

One of the most striking moves in the development of our metrological concepts is to look to nature for an immutable standard. With the metric system, the basic unit of measurement was at first based on the length of one minute of arc of the circumference of the Earth, whereas now the basic unit of length is based on "1,650,753.37 wave lengths of the orange light emitted by the Krypton atom of mass 86 *in vacus*." "We have gone a long way from the measures of the feudal epoch that meant so much in human terms," Kula writes. "Yet, at the same time, the process has taken us very far along the road of more effective and fruitful international understanding and cooperation" (1986, 121).

In particular, the development of an abstract standard based on objective and practically unchanging natural phenomenon is connected in important ways with the development of society and its economic and political structures. For a society to be "able to adopt measures of pure convention, two important conditions have first to be satisfied: there must prevail a de facto equality of men before the law, and there must be accomplished the process of alienation of the commodity" (Kula, 1986, 122), in other words the economic and political relations of capitalism. The presence of different laws for different people means different measures for different people.[5] Kula states, "Inequality before the law implies unequal laws or rights in relation to measures: some people decree them, others have to put up with them; everyone has a measure of his own, the strong imposing theirs upon the weak" (122). He also says that the measure is not impersonal, but human; "it belongs to some, it does not belong to others, and it is dependent upon the will of whoever has the power to enforce it." Not until there is "equality before the law can there be metrological equality. The measure will then cease to depend on anyone's will, and this will symbolize its 'kinship' with the dimensions of the terrestrial globe—for, after all, no one can exercise an influence over that" (122). Might we hypothesize that measures of the natural world be rooted in nature, while measures of the social world be rooted in society?

Again, where to place the standardized test in the context of the "standards movement"? Certainly reformers speak of one standard for all as a basis for equality, a good example being federal mandates to include special education students in state testing schemes and "disaggregate" data by social categories. Yet it is clear that the standard is predicated on the will of an authority that has the power to impose it, that many "have to put up with" it, a fact that signifies great inequality. It is also clear that the present circumstance bears no resemblance to a "terrestrial globe" and, far from being public and an objective natural phenomenon, test secrecy, waivers, mishaps, and exclusive control by publishing monopolies is the norm. This points to the significance of standardization and its relationship to notions of democracy, equality, and the public.

Power, Equality, and the Standardization of Measures

Standardization has several meanings in the context of education. One notion is simply that all students are treated equally throughout the testing situation and given the same test. The results of the test are rendered using the same scoring rubric. Hence the second definition of standardization offered by the OED is "To test by a standard." The aim of standardized educational assessment is to compare students to the same standard (equality before the law). Giving rich and poor kids the same test is a reflection of the egalitarian movement as it developed in the West, and, of course, reveals the limits of that movement. Standardization refers to the successful application of a standard, "the condition in which a standard has been achieved or effectively applied," according to Webster's. In this sense it would be hard to have standards without standardization, and it is hard to imagine a standard being "effectively applied" without enforcement.

Kula shows that for centuries, authorities at various levels sought to standardize their measures as part of unifying their territory or expanding their control over new territory. Commercial interests, the drive to unify the nation, and anti-aristocratic drives have historically driven most standardization efforts (1986, 192). This notion of standardization, however, contrasts with the one accompanying the development of the metric system. "The pre-metric standardization of the eighteenth century did not seek universality; on the contrary, the objective was, as it had been since the Carolingians, that measures should be identified with the ruler and be coextensive with his rule. Universal, mankind-wide objectives were yet to make their appearance—as a concomitant of the metric reforms" (Kula 1986, 118). What is significant about universalism in political terms is (1) its connection to equality before the law, and (2) the concurrent claim of neutrality. Unlike monarchic forms of standardization, a universal system of standards is accepted by and adhered to by all parties; this is given as fair and impartial, as existing above class conflict, and a means to sort out conflicts.

In the context of defending standardized tests, and the College Board exams in particular, Wooten presents the argument of then-College Board President George Hanford: "Admissions tests provide a uniform measure of intellectual readiness for academic work at the college level." Such test scores, Wooten argues, should "provide a more uniform basis on which to evaluate academic ability and achievement than do other measures such as grades" (1982, 11–12). While this practice is justified on the basis that different school districts offer different curriculums and that teachers' grades are not comparable, I think this may only partly explain these practices.

Comparability and uniformity are key in that power is required to enforce one standard of judgment, thus making evaluation uniform and hence equitable. Witness how accountability is presented. Wiggins defines accountability as "comparability on common measures" (1993, 15). While arguing for standards-based reform, IBM's John Akers presents a similar view, arguing, "accountability is rooted in the idea of measurement" (quoted in Shaker 1998, 17). Standardization means comparability on common measures. Such standardization functions to make those who have the standard applied to them accountable to those who set the standard, emphasizing the role standards play in obtaining power. In this sense, standardized norm-referenced tests are monarchical, not modern or universal as the metric system.

The question then is not so much whether standardization is "bad" or "good" but whose interests does such standardization serve, what outlook does it reflect, and so on. What is often confused in the critical discourse about standardization is that because standardization can mean "to bring to a standard or uniform size, strength, form of construction, proportion of ingredients, or the like" the aim of standardized testing or standards-based reform is often given as producing uniformity. Hence the objections that standards-based reformers impose conformity, the total loss of individuality (e.g., Meier 2000; Wiggins 1991). But the aim of "testing by a standard" is not standardization of that which is tested, but uniform differentiation. This is a variant of equal treatment consistent with the democratic norm of political equality. In educational assessment, it is not the standardization of students, but rather the standardization of measurers that is at issue, a standardization that bolsters a central power, its aim, outlook, and so on.

For liberal democratic theory, the process of applying the same standard uniformly to a population enables social differentiation of individuals and groups to take place on a uniform (and hence fair) basis. This type of standardization has medieval roots, since it retains the fixation on social hierarchies. It is a standardization that is not consistent with the modern metric system.

As odd as it may seem to the reader, to offer as critique of standardized testing the observation that all are not provided equal resources prior to testing misses the central role of nature in this theory: resources are a basis for social distinction and hence should not be considered! By applying the same standard to all students, ranked categories of performance can be established, that is, vertical classification on a natural basis. To demand social equality as a starting point eliminates the possibility of vertical classification. Ranking performance of individuals would, by virtue of logic, not result in a hierarchy of groups of human beings, since the original assumption of social equality eliminates this possibility. The equalization of resources makes no sense to the prevailing political theory. Equalization of resources is premised on an entirely different social aim, the project of eliminating social classes. Few Enlightenment thinkers sought social equality, and certainly neoliberals will block any policy that even suggests eliminating social distinction!

A third, equally important consideration is the degree to which the standard is public. Feudal arrangements had it so that lords would retain custody of the standards, making it their prerogative to benefit from the monopoly over standards through leasing of weights and measure; the similarities to the present standards-based movement's link to big publishing companies is striking (Pile 2005). It was in their interests to use different standards for different purposes—buying and selling, or collecting taxes—

and during the rise of absolutism in Europe, there emerged a struggle between the lords and the king on this question. But in either case, neither arrangement requires that the standards be public, the corollary of which would be that all (including the authority) are subject to the same standards, or, again, equality before the law, a conception anathema to feudal systems. Indeed, one of the demands leading up to the French Revolution was on this question of "laying open the lords' measures" (Kula 1986, 197). In this way, open or public standards are bound up with equality before the law, both of which stand against arbitrary power and recognize the public as a valid political category.

While it is clear that the emergence of industrialization made a clear break with feudal practices, the status of our political and social practices in this regard is the source of much of the present difficulty. In other words, our present political and social institutions have yet to break with key aspects of feudal society. In modern forms of production, standardization refers to uniformity, and without uniformity of this type, one could not have industrialization or the material abundance it yields. One should be very careful about social critique that identifies standardization as *the* problem. In political terms standardization does not mean producing uniformity as much as it means ignoring difference. For example, a basic democratic precept is that all citizens—irrespective of wealth or income; religion, language, or culture; sexuality or skin color—are to be treated as equals in political terms, that is, they are equal before the law, have equal rights and duties as citizens, and so on.

Today the social significance of academic ranking, whether among individuals or subject areas for one individual, is competition. This is the essence of equal opportunity, where the test is constituted as the "equal playing field"; all are treated the same by the test and this is what makes that form of power fair. While equality before the law may be premised on ignoring difference, an equal playing field exists to rank difference (political equality does not equal fair competition or differentiation). Thus, to summarize, standardization has a distinct meaning and function in terms of economic production, one different from the realm of politics under capitalism. And in terms of political conceptions, the rise of bourgeois democracy gives rise to equality before the law and notions of equal opportunity or fair competition. Industrial production requires uniformity; political notions of equal opportunity produce ranked difference by the uniform application of the same standard to individuals or groups. The latter clearly values ranked social difference while the former does not. This is, in fact, one of the key contradictions inherent to capitalism.

Thus, interestingly enough, opposition to standardization has historically resided in opposition to "leveling." "Finally," Kula writes after introducing the various functional and symbolic roles of standards, "it seems worthwhile to ponder certain anti-egalitarian connotations, not so much of measures as of the process of measuring, especially the practice of leveling or striking," which appears as an early effort at standardization of the measuring process. He offers the following, which speaks of opposition to standardization as an egalitarian project. "Idiomatic phrases for employing one standard for all are found universally, and Kohlberg has reported the analogous and more pithy formulated Polish proverb: 'Stick your head out of the bushel and you'll get it leveled by the strickle'" (Kula 1986, 12). Again, this anti-egalitarian notion can be seen in public policy debates when it is claimed that standardized tests crush individual initiative and creativity.

All this suggests that standardization as taken up in education is political in nature, revealed in its connection with social differentiation on the one hand, and the problems surrounding egalitarian projects on the other. Opposing standardization as such without a careful investigation of these issues may be a tacit call for premodern and categorically unequal social relations characteristic of feudal arrangements. As I will argue in the chapter 9, the problem is not so much with standardization as with the historical limits of the notions of equality and rights that came into being with the modern nation state.

The Heuristic Outlined

Standard setting and control over standards are means of ruling and governing, and thus any study examining the origins and significance of any particular standard should take into account the political significance of standards and standard setting. Tools used to measure or assess (testing instruments) can be studied according to how they establish and serve an authority, and embody its political theory and social values. Such knowledge is likely to be revealed by examining struggles to bring about new standards, struggles that include the wrecking and discrediting of old standards and the systems and power of which they were a part. In what way do new standards, or at least old standards controlled by a different authority, represent or constitute significant changes in power relations, political theory, and the social value system?

In summary then, this guide poses the following questions when examining the origin of standards, such as the standardized test of achievement or ability:

- How do struggles over standards reflect political struggles, within or between classes? Does a change in standards, or who controls the standard, relate to changes in governance? What is the theory of power embodied in the standard?

- How and why did an existing or aspiring authority make measures mandatory, retain custody of standards, or punish any "metrological transgressions"? Did failure to enforce and retain such standards suggest a loss of power or legitimacy?
- How and why did an existing or aspiring authority seek to unify all measures within its territory, or in new territories?
- In what ways do the new standards embody the social values of the authority's class or faction?

These themes run together and ultimately must be considered as one dynamic. The aim is to delineate a method of consideration, a set of themes by which to explore the various aspects of educational assessment.

3

Academic Achievement and Ability as Forms of Vertical Classification

If standards setting and control over standards are connected with ruling and governing, key aspects of any new standards would appear with the emergence of a new social order. Underpinning standardized academic tests are the notions of achievement and ability that emerged with the rise of the modern nation state and in particular the theory of government by "virtue and talent." Achievement and ability are explored here as social values.

The notion of social value, derived from one of the founders of sociology, Emile Durkheim, signifies how value is socially attached to groups as well as to structural positions via status duality (good or bad) and spatial duality (high or low). This duality of the good and the bad, the high and the low constitutes the two levels of value duality within a system of vertical classification or ranked categories. Within such a system, all individuals and groups are then placed in either the sacred or the profane position; theoretically, they are mutually exclusive categories. Vertical classification is necessarily connected to physical and moral power since moral value and structural position are presented as correlates. The assignment of individuals to unequal structural positions within a social system is a use of power that generates the conditions for structural inequality (Williams 1990, 1–6).

These words—*genius*, *moron*, *gifted*, and so on—especially the more demeaning ones, are often, and rightly so, placed in scare quotes. But here I want to retain such words because they are markers of social value. The classification systems used by psychologists and psychiatrists during the emergence of psychometry as a discipline was expressly value laden and signifies how value can be socially attached to groups as well as to structural positions. This is not only evidenced by the common reaction to the use of these words today, but by their etymology: *morons* (the foolish or dull), *idiots* (persons without professional knowledge, ignorant persons, common men), and *imbeciles* (the weak minded).[1] Even when psychometricians have explicitly taken a technical stance toward the word *intelligence*, putatively striving to differentiate it from common usage, they end up speaking about gifted and bright children, as well as dull and stupid children; one cannot enter a school and fail to hear talk of good and bad students. While possibly offered as a basis for the criticism of psychometry, foremost these words signify the real aim of psychometry—the determination of social value and mystification of historically structured inequality.[2]

Individual and group value are linked to the value of the structural position each occupies in the society. Wall Street moguls, corporate CEOs, and policy experts constitute the apex of value, while, for example, immigrant farmworkers, drug addicts, and the homeless occupy the base of value, its bottom point. In the case of educational achievement and ability, this linkage is made possible by standards developed according to the prevailing mode of social organization and the attending value system. When social value links structural position with individuals and their group identity in the context of the ideology of merit, such linkages make possible and ideologically acceptable the practice of giving more to those who already have, for those who are of most value also "deserve" the most. That is, the social value system is the basis on which legitimation and justification of various forms of inequality take place.

In education, social value is evident both in the classification of individuals and groups in terms of success or failure and "good" and "bad" forms of pedagogy, curriculum, and school organization, as three pertinent examples. The provision of different types of pedagogy and curricula, often within the same school building, signify social positions (modes of socialization) in the sense that working-class students often receive "basic skills training" while their middle-class peers are engaged in art and science projects and enriching field trips; children of the elite attend schools that prepare them for power. With this the value of the training is connected with the value of the student or their group identity. In the current social system, professionals and their children are valued more than workers and their children, the evidence of which is the social status and power afforded these two different groups. The spirit in which some youth refer to remedial placements, such as "retard," are less signs of immaturity and more signs of their internalization of the prevailing social values system.[3] This duality of the sacred and the profane—say, the gifted and the retarded—thus constitutes the two levels of value duality within a system of vertical classification, or ranked categories.

Thus, it seems to me that marking virtue (good or bad) and talent (high or low) constitute the object of standardized test-based assessment within a hierarchically structured social system premised on the idea of merit—that one's position in the hierarchy is earned or deserved, where rich and powerful is morally "good" and poor and powerless is morally "bad". With this understanding, educational testing appears as an elegant example of vertical classification.

As I will explore more in chapter 5, achievement and ability are given in Western political thought as a "natural" basis for the vertical classification of human beings. In a society that rejects rule by bloodlines but affirms the rule of private property, "natural" forms of vertical classification of human beings are given as justification for extant inequality.[4]

There are two notions of natural here that need to be explored. The formation of vertical classification systems themselves distorts social reality by rendering the human group as a series of separate categories that are internally homogeneous—different categories are presented as if they exist prior to or outside of society, that is, as natural. In this way, vertical classification is the underlying logical basis of racism, for it divides the human group into ranked classes of value. Whether this marking takes place on the basis of skin color or intellectual ability matters little in terms of the underlying logic. Note as well that the issue is not mainly whether ability or achievement is given as primarily due to genetics or the environment. The argument here is that the vertical classification resulting from standardized tests presupposes achievement and ability rankings as natural, that is, as distinct from the artificial (or social) distinctions of social class. In other words, to talk about individual achievement and ability in a hierarchically structured society such as ours is to suggest that these categories of achievement and ability and the predictable patterns they yield exist prior to or outside of the historically structured inequality in which individuals are, in fact, located. This talk of ability and achievement thus aims at the impossible: the liberation of individuals from their social roots. But the fact is that achievement and ability rankings are themselves socially structured and patterned phenomena and no amount of attitude adjustment among teachers and students will change this structurally determined reality.

In education, ability and achievement exist as relational concepts (low ability has meaning relative only to high ability). Achievement is in our culture competitive, and thus relational, as winner is to loser. Yet at the moment the division between high and low ability or achievement is made, the designation becomes absolute: each individual (or group) can be in only one category, "hence that absolute perception of vertical classification abstracts people from the flux of their history" (Williams 1990, 2). It is this process of abstraction that contributes to an understanding of ability and achievement as a natural (i.e., nonsocial) basis for the classification of the human population. This is significant because designations of natural stand as a nonbiased means by which to classify human beings.

Note in particular that this notion of natural distinction is the premise of equity or fairness as framed in educational policy. It is the project of establishing social inequality on the basis of natural distinction that American revolutionaries claimed the mantel of "land of opportunity" and "equality and justice for all" for the United States. Notions of ability and achievement were instrumental for this project and the forming of the U.S. political order. The limits (and evident failure) of these inherited and politicized notions of ability and achievement, especially as they serve to guide the organization of education, are striking when examined from this point of view.

Again the notion of natural here is in contradiction to social and need not (of course it often does) reference the biological proper. That the marks of ability and achievement are not stable in the way skin pigment or biological sex are helps explain why testing has historically been given such an extensive role in the United States: each test is an opportunity to be marked as worthy in rank and thus a basis for making claims on society. More testing equals more opportunity. For those at the bottom of the social order, each test is a chance to break free of their social roots by proving their "natural" abilities, as if Darwin discovered obscure word analogies as a basis for natural selection! Also suggested by this observation is the idea that discussions about achievement and ability differences by group (sex, race, or social class) are extremely significant, that ability and achievement are presently racist conceptions in that they presume a hierarchy of worth among presumed categories of human beings.

4

Standardized Tests as Markers of Social Value

Whether one is a student in college to obtain their bachelor's of science in psychology, a superintendent preparing a report to a school board, or a university admissions officer, data collected from educational and psychological tests are typically emphasized. The results of intelligence tests (ability or IQ) are said to measure student intelligence, achievement tests are presented as measurements of subject mastery and the basis for judging the relative performance of schools and school districts, and entrance exams are given as measurements of ability to succeed in college, to take only three common examples. The words *measure, measures,* or *measurement* appear, by my count, at least 135 times throughout the federal No Child Left Behind Act, the provisions of which rely more than in any other time on the results of standardized tests. It is widely believed that this law represents a fundamental change in the structure and function of education in the United States, with test scores constituting a key mechanism to bring about and justify this change (Conley 2003). But what if educational and psychological tests and the data they yield are not measurements at all?

The assumption that psychological and educational tests measure something is as old as the tests themselves, and it is an assumption that is rarely if ever challenged. Although it is noteworthy that Alfred Binet, the inventor of what is known as the IQ test, acknowledged that his test was not, in fact, a measurement, he nonetheless continued to speak about and present his instrument as just that: a scale for the measurement of intelligence. "The scale properly speaking," Binet and Simon wrote, "does not permit the measure of the intelligence, because intellectual qualities are not superposable, and therefore cannot be measured as linear surfaces are measured, but are on the contrary, a classification, a hierarchy among diverse intelligences," but, they continue, "for the necessities of practice

this classification is equivalent to a measure" (Binet and Simon 1916, 41).[1]
Foreshadowing arguments of future psychometricians, they justified this
inconsistency by claiming—without explanation—that it was of practical
necessity. Yet classification by level of performance would have served
Binet and Simon's stated purpose of identifying those who will not benefit from "regular" instruction most adequately. It was not the necessities
of practice but the necessities of theory that led Binet to announce his invention of a "metric scale of intelligence." Had he admitted that children
were merely classified by level of performance (or even by level of mental
development) there would have been no basis on which to account for
school attainment in terms of measured intelligence (Nash 1990).

That an entire field (what is referred to here as psychometry) could be
granted so much authority and financial support, at least in part on the basis
of measurement, with evident uncertainty of what is being measured is, in
fact, baffling and, in my view, perversely irrational. How is it that so many
of us have taken for granted that measurement is taking place when there is
so much disagreement over what is being measured? It may, in fact, be the
case that this assumption of measurement has enabled psychometric practice
to withstand periodic, intense, and what now appears to be mounting criticism. Constructing alternatives to psychometric practice, in turn, depends
on efforts to reexamine the significance and legitimacy of psychometry's
claims to measurement and the nature of assessment more generally.

Popularized critiques of testing assume that a key problem lies with the
misuse of educational and psychological tests and specious interpretations
of the meaning of test scores. For example, so-called hereditarians use the
same standard—the IQ test—as so-called environmentalists do; the rub is
in the use and interpretation of scores. One group posits the primacy of
genes in differential academic performance between so-called races; the
other retorts that such group differences in test scores prove the negative im-
pacts of poverty and discrimination on intellectual development. Psychometric practice has actually flourished in this context, eagerly developing
concepts and methods—such as construct validation—for determining the
proper use and meaning of test scores, a project that garners further institutional and fiscal backing. Psychometry's response to these challenges over
the past four decades has also served as a basis on which to maintain its legitimacy as a science and thus its instructional power (see Nash 1990).

In this chapter, I suggest a different direction. I argue that psychometry
fails to meet its claim of measurement and that its object is not the measurement of nonphysical human attributes, but the marking of some human
beings as having more worth or value than other human beings, an act central to and part and parcel of the legitimacy of a particular kind of hierarchical social system known as capitalism, and in particular its political shell,
representative democracy. Psychometry's claim to measurement serves to

veil and justify the fundamentally political act of marking social value, and the role this practice plays in legitimating vast social inequalities.

Definitions of Psychometry

According to the Oxford English Dictionary, *psychometry* literally means measuring the soul, or "mind measuring." The first reported use of the word, appearing in 1854, gave psychometry as the "faculty of divining, from physical contact or proximity only, the qualities or properties of an object, or of persons or things that have been in contact with it." Sense two is given as follows: "The measurement of the duration and intensity of mental states or processes" with the following quote from Francis Galton. "Psychometry . . . means the art of imposing measurement and number upon operations of the mind, as in the practice of determining the reaction-time of different persons." (Galton's choice of the word *imposing* should not go unnoticed.) And finally, the OED offers this definition for psychometrics, one with a more contemporary flare: "The science of measuring mental capacities and processes; the application of methods of measurement to the various branches of psychology."

The literal, etymological meaning of psychometry is a useful place to begin. What would it mean to measure mind (or soul for that matter)? Is mind the kind of thing one has more or less of? Or, to start with the more contemporary definition, are mental capacities such that they exist in gradation? Is a theory of mind needed to determine if mind can be measured, and if so, how metrication can take place? The issues raised here are fundamental from the point of view of both the theory and practice of measurement, and addressing them serves as a useful starting point for deliberating on the nature of measurement and the status of psychometry as a science.

One possible reason for the absence of a broad discussion among academics and the public concerning measurement of nonphysical entities is that the limited amount of material available on this question is highly technical. Fundamental problems in the philosophy of science such as the nature of knowledge and scientific objectivity are at issue; ability (and or willingness) to contend with complex mathematics is also typically required. Yet it is possible to develop a broad and accessible discussion of measurement. It is also the case that psychometricians generally avoid the problems posed by measurement of nonphysical entities in the name of being practical. But we must ask: what practical problem is solved by rendering psychological and educational tests as measurements? In this regard, it is absolutely necessary to go into the nature of measurement if so much of educational reform is contingent on the results of what are given as measurements. A final difficulty with this topic is the language itself, where the word *measure* has numerous meanings and uses in the English language.

The Nature of Measurement

Measurement deals with the dialectical relationship between quantity and quality. The central theoretical concept of measurement is magnitude, defined as the property of relative size or extent. Simply stated, measurement deals with the question of how much or magnitude. We may also distinguish between discrete and continuous magnitudes. The former is obtained by empirical methods, the latter theoretical. For example the length of the diagonal of a square equals the square root of the sum of their squares, yet this value cannot be obtained by empirical procedures, only by calculation (Berka 1983; Nash 1990).

The common expression "how much" suggests the dialectical unity of quantity and quality in measurement. A magnitude (which is represented by a standard) is a known quality that is also known to exist in degrees. Measurement is integral to determining points at which quantitative change leads to change in quality (for example, the point at which an increase in heat transforms water into steam). Psychometric efforts to determine at what point scores on a particular test make a person qualified represent this logic, even if the reality is that what are known as cut scores are arbitrarily determined.

A standard is a tool used in assessment, comparison, and measurement. Common, everyday standards of length and weight represent known magnitudes. Yet, a standard, for example the meter, must be theoretically and technically fit for the measure of objectively existing properties of a thing or phenomenon. Once accomplished, this allows for different objects, processes, or phenomena to be compared in relation to the same magnitude, such as weight, length, heat, and so forth. It is also the standard that allows for equivalence, or calibration.

It is important to emphasize that while a standard is necessary for measurement, at least initial theoretical work is presupposed for it to be able to accurately represent magnitudes. For example, there needed to be a conception of the qualitative aspect of heat before its measurement could take place. Once such theoretical knowledge is at least initially established measurement becomes possible (Block and Dworkin 1976). The centrality of theory to measurement is contrary to the practice of psychometry, in which the "meaning" of test scores is derived after the fact, via methods of correlation with other tests, and the like. In fact, some have gone as far as to suggest no definition (let alone a theory) of intelligence is needed for its measure and hence the mind-numbing proposition that intelligence is the ability to do well on an intelligence test is presented as acceptable practice to generations of psychology students (see Block and Dworkin 1976). A century has gone by "measuring" intelligence with no proven theory and "measuring" achievement with little consensus on curricular domains or a theory of human cognitive development. Again, proceeding without resolving this problem is justified on the basis of "practical" necessity! What kind of practice is it that vociferously shuns theory as the basis for its science?

Contrary to what seems to be conventional wisdom, the level of precision is not the key to measurement. The claim to measurement is the claim that laws governing quantitative and qualitative change can be accurately represented mathematically. This is the criterion of being isomorphic. For a measurement system to be valid there must be a correspondence between elements, relations, and operations of the mathematical and substantive system in question. This correspondence is exemplified with the additive principle: one can take ten feet and add it to ten feet and obtain twenty feet. Notice that individual test items cannot be shown to be equivalent in this manner. While there are exceptions to the universality of the additive principle for measurement (e.g., with heat phenomena), the example stands for my purposes here (Berka 1983; Nash 1990).[2]

Psychometry, in contradiction to this definition, renders measurement as the mere application of number systems to objects, processes or phenomena, a process that has no necessary reference to the empirical world (see Lorge [1951] 1996). This is the notion of measurement as social convention. Many critics have thus designated psychometry as "measurement by fiat" (Cicourel 1964; also see Block and Dworkin 1976; Pawson, 1989). Without too much difficulty, one can find psychometricians admitting that the ability of test scores to truthfully reflect quantities of a characteristic of interest is suspect.[3]

If psychometry's definition is accepted as the basis for practice, any rule-based assignment of numbers to phenomena could claim measurement. Common practice in the social sciences has it that a questionnaire, for example, in which the respondent expresses his or her attitude with the aid of numbers, is an instance of measurement of preferences (Berka 1970, 1983; Nash, 1990).[4]

In addition to the idealist assumptions underpinning psychometry's definition of measurement is the field's tendency to imbue data with properties of the testing procedure. One cannot assume a scale to be a property of that which is measured if that scale is a necessary consequence of the method of analysis (Cicourel 1964, 13). The relevance here to educational and psychological testing is striking. It is not permissible to argue that intelligence (or any purported characteristic of individuals) is normally distributed in a population on the basis of the normal distribution of scores because a normal distribution is demanded by the statistical methods most commonly used in test construction and analysis. While "such a procedure ought to be virtually standard practice by the lights of many current parametric techniques," Pawson writes, "to do so . . . is a 'gratuitous' expression of statistical expedience" (1986, 56).

Most importantly for our purposes here, theoretical work determines if the property or quality under investigation can be measured. The development of measurement has generally progressed from classification based on quality to topology or the comparison of qualitative aspects of phenomena to metrication and thus measurement. Classification concepts such as "cold" become topological when comparisons (such as "colder than . . .") are used. Such concepts not only establish sameness (or difference), but also make it possible to compare at least two objects that possess a given property; this in turn makes it possible to arrange such objects into a sequence (Berka 1983). Given the difficulties associated with their methodology, questionnaires, to continue with the previous example, are at best topological in nature.

While topological concepts provide a possible transition from classification to measurement, it is important to note that classification (or differentiation) itself is not measurement. This is contrary to what is commonly asserted in contemporary textbooks on psychological and educational testing (e.g., Hopkins, Stanley, and Hopkins 1990, 1–3). The ability to differentiate and rank on the basis of common properties does not in itself allow one to claim that the extent of that property can be determined. In this way, the common presentation in social science texts of levels of measurement—nominal, ordinal, and so on—makes the fundamental error of presuming mere classification to be a form of measurement. But classification is not a level of measurement.

Thus, a key problem, one I pointed to with the definition of psychometry as mind measurement, is the assumption that the mind or a purported faculty or function of mind is a property capable of gradation. There are, however, many properties that do not permit gradation (i.e., they are not magnitudes) such as *Pilsner, feline, wooden,* and *human.* In other words, the psychometric dictum of E. L. Thorndike (the famous early-twentieth-century psychometrician) that "whatever exists at all exists in some amount" is patently false (as quoted in Haney 1977, 12).

Yet, Thorndike's premise has great social and political significance. We know that human history is riddled with cases of some humans beings designated as less human, or not human at all; humanness has been given as something individual persons and groups have more or less of—a key presupposition of the eugenicist's project of a "master race." The U.S. Constitution made this presumption when it rendered African slaves and Native peoples as only holding a fraction of the value of white Europeans. Such designations were based on the claim that some human beings have less intelligence, ability, or otherwise valued attribute, than other human beings, and on that basis, they were rendered less human, of less value, and, in some cases, a threat to civilization itself. Such designations served to justify inequalities and crimes associated with slavery, colonialism, and capitalism.

Most readers, however, will accept at some level that education is something that can be graded. Clearly, some students learn more of a particular subject matter than others, and, clearly, people obtain, both officially and in practice, different levels of education or expertise in different fields, and so on. In this way, measuring educational achievement seems less problematic than measuring mind or intelligence. Defining content areas such as math and delineating levels of mathematical knowledge seem relatively simple by comparison.

The project of measuring academic knowledge in practice, however, appears particularly fixated on ranking human beings and less on determining degrees of knowledge per se. For example, norm-referenced achievement tests offer results in terms of percentile ranks, not delineations of what a student does or does not know about a given field of study, let alone diagnoses of the cause of any difficulty. Put another way, scoring in the seventieth percentile only indicates how well one did relative to the norm; it does not indicate 70 percent of required material was mastered. Thus, the test remains at the topological level, where percentile results indicate only that, for example, Sue performed better than Joe; the preceding semantics suggest that the object is, in fact, the ranking of the worth or value of persons, and not what they know or can do as such. It is not uncommon to hear educators move from reporting student grades to designations of students as "good" and "bad," suggesting that differential academic performance reflects some moral order. Using a previously cited example, if one says "colder than . . ." the comparison is in terms of temperature; to say "better than . . ." suggests comparison is in terms of worth, where grades and tests scores are the currency by which such value is negotiated and ultimately exchanged.

The same problem exists with so-called measurements of ability. By virtue of being norm-referenced, such tests only provide rank order information on the basis of students' ability to furnish what are considered correct responses to test prompts. This ranking does not in any way permit the claim that "cognitive ability" is therefore being measured because ranking is itself not measurement (Nash 1990, 63). In this way, present-day achievement and ability tests cannot measure any property of individuals or groups: their object is to rank order the value of individuals and groups.

State tests that mark school and district proficiency level also reflect this problem—these levels or benchmarks cannot be shown to correspond in a consistent and sufficiently precise way to an actual body of knowledge or set of skills (Haney 2000; also see Bracey 2002, 21–26).

Because standardized achievement tests take as their object the differentiation and ranking of human persons, and not what has actually been learned by students as a result of instruction, some testing experts have argued such tests should not be used for accountability purposes (Popham 1999; Wesson 2000).

A further difficulty lies in the fact that there is no evidence that the numbers produced (test scores) correspond to (are isomorphic with) what we understand to be laws governing mental processes and functions, or the dialectical relationship between qualitative and quantitative aspects of these processes or functions.

Thus, as there is no proof to being isomorphic with the object of measurement, let alone a defined object of measurement, educational and psychological tests cannot claim to reflect laws and rules governing psychological processes, for the "necessary conditions for metrication do not exist" (Nash 1990, 145).

Ranking human worth on the basis of how well one competes in academic contests, with the effect that high ranks are associated with privilege, status, and power, does suggest that psychometry is best explored as a form of vertical classification and attending rankings of social value.

Validity

In traditional psychometric theory, validity is defined as the degree to which a test measures what it claims to measure. I want to first point out the oddity of this formulation. For example, how does the reader respond to this: My ruler is valid to the degree to which it measures length. Is it normal practice to validate a ruler by asking this seemingly circular question? Rulers by definition measure length. Possibly more important here is the fact that by asking what a test measures the assumption that something is being measured goes unchallenged.

The importance of theory is revealed in sorting this out for in reality a ruler is a standard of length, just as my forearm, the meter, and the inch are standards of length. My forearm does not measure length any less or more than the inch—both can determine the length of an object. Just to make the point clear, my forearm may be longer or shorter than the reader's, yet both can measure that property called length.

There are generally four types of test validation: predictive, concurrent, content, and construct. Nash's work (1990) renders a powerful critique of the psychometric discourse of validity, while others have analyzed the persistent confusion between facts and values (Block and Dowrkin 1976; Schiff and Lewontin 1986). However, for the purposes here, I want to emphasize validity discourse as a form of justification. According to Wilson, the

American Psychological Association's standards state: "Validity is the most important consideration in test evaluation. The concept refers to the appropriateness, meaningfulness, and usefulness of the specific inferences made from test scores." It goes on immediately to explain that "test validation is the process of accumulating evidence to support such inferences" (1998, chap. 16, ¶15). Two things stand out here. First, how is it possible that the meaning of any test lies somewhere outside the test? Nash warns that "the view that meaning lies anywhere other than in the test-text must be resisted" (1990, 133). If the test-text does not contain the meaning of the test—many students and teachers feel such tests are indeed meaningless—then it is not possible for the test taker to grasp the meaning of the test. Intervention of specially trained judges (experts), who will decide the meaning of the test for the taker and the consumer of that information, is thus required and justified. This brings us to the second point, which is that "accumulating evidence to support such inferences" is unabashedly what Wilson calls advocacy. He explains, "The 1985 Guidelines describes an ideal validation as including several types of evidence." "However," the American Psychological Association's manual emphasizes, "the quality of the evidence is of primary importance, and a single line of solid evidence is preferable to numerous lines of evidence of questionable validity." Wilson rightly points to the "tautology and redundancy in the phrase questionable validity" as "remarkably inept." But even more significant is this:

> [V]alidity is proposed as the characteristic of the evidence used to support the construct "validity," and the essence of the concept is surely its very questionability. Far more damning, however, is the clear implication that evidence that does not cogently support the assertions of the test users should not be presented. Putting it another way, validity is a concept based on advocacy, is a rationalizing tool for a methodological decision already made, and is an ideological support rather than a scientific enterprise. (1998, chap. 16, ¶14–15)

Thus, with this, the project of psychometry is properly understood as political theory, for it serves to justify decisions regarding the position of people and allocation of resources within a system of structured inequality.

Standardized Tests Are Standards for Assessment, Not Measurement

Assessment appears focused on determining quality (as in designations of good, authentic, etc.). Even the notion of "good enough" appears as qualitative in nature (as opposed to "how much"), and is properly identified as a judgment, not a measurement. While it is common to suggest that measurement is simply a more precise form of assessment (e.g. Hopkins, Stanley, and Hopkins 1990)—not to mention that the words *measure* and *assess* are given as synonyms in many thesauruses—more than levels of precision distinguish assessment from measurement.

For almost the duration of their six hundred years in use, the words *assess* and *assessment* have been employed in discussions of taxation, tributes, and fines. It is not until the nineteenth century that assessment is used in the general sense as a synonym for estimation or evaluation. And it is only with the institutionalization of the fields of education and psychology in the twentieth century that the now common meaning of *assessment* is derived. Thus, it is only by the fifth definition that the OED defines assessment as an educational endeavor: "The process or means of evaluating academic work; an examination or test." Interestingly, the word *assessment* is presented as almost synonymous with the word *examination* or *test*. And the increasingly practical role psychology played in contemporary institutions gave rise to notions of assessment as this one: "To evaluate (a person or thing); to estimate (the quality, value, or extent of), to gauge or judge." Examining the development of the use of the word further, the OED offers this quote from the Office of Strategic Services' 1948 publication, *Assessment of Men*: "A number of psychologists and psychiatrists attempted to assess the merits of men and women recruited for the Office of Strategic Services." In this way, assessment has historically related to judgments of value (originally in the form of taxation) with the more recent developments specific to judging the value or deservedness of human beings on the basis of academic performance and psychological profile.

Further examination of the word suggests that not only is it bound up with judging human value in particular, but it also explicitly recognizes social hierarchy as a variable. *Assess* is a form of the Latin verb meaning "to sit with." In an educational assessment, the assessor sits with the learner and assigns value. In this way, assessment is predicated on human relationships in a way that measurement is not. The word's alternative meaning clearly suggests the importance of social position when it states that this person who "sits beside" (as in an assistant-judge) is one who "shares another's rank or dignity" and who is "skilled to advise on technical points" (Wiggins 1993). It is also important to point out that assessments are connected to what is called "professional judgment," a notion that is connected to authority and autonomy from bureaucratic supervision.

Measurement takes *magnitude* as its object, the abstract (mathematical) expression of the extent of qualities of things or phenomena. Assessment takes *value* as its object. Value requires a valuing subject and an object to be valued. Relationships of this type are often political because the act of valuing often invokes power; certainly assessing property values in the form of taxes is political, that is, requires power. With measurement, standards make possible the grasping of the relation between quality and quantity. Standards in assessment make possible the judgment of value by stipulating boundary points or indices as indicators of quality (merit, worth, goodness, authenticity). My point here is to argue that official educational assessment operates on the basis of establishing desired qualities and their vertical classification, or the placement of individuals into ranked categories, with the assistance of numbers such that they correspond with existing social structures (which is given as evidence that they are "valid"). The validity discourse about test score meaning relative to testing purpose reveals that the value in the form of achievement and ability does not reside in things or phenomena themselves, but in their relation to subjects. Length, for example, is a property of an object. Thus, we can delineate standards in measurement as absolute or universal, while standards in assessment are relative or topological (see chapter 1).

The issue is not to privilege measurement or to denigrate judgment—nor is it a claim that judgments are subjective in the pejorative sense (one could have objective criteria for judgment, in that all could see and apply the criteria); humans could not live without judgment of some kind (see Broadfoot 1979). The point is simply to identify the phenomenon under investigation; namely, standardized tests are forms of assessment, the object of which is to categorically rank the presumed difference in the value or worth of human persons. But worth or value does not originate in things or phenomenon themselves. It originates in the structure of relationships. Something is valuable to someone for some purpose. The notion of race, for example, has no meaning outside a ranked category system with mutually exclusive poles. It is impossible to determine the social meaning of one "race" outside its relation to other races as per some (literally) racist schema. Standards used in measurement do not have this quality.

The confusion between measurement and assessment is thus not insignificant, having both scientific and ideological importance. A common error is the confusion of the properties of objects with the properties of numbers and social relations and the properties of those objects or phenomena in the relation. A good example of this error is rendering the ranking of individuals as the measurement of their ability. Presenting assessments as measurements functions to mask the workings of the values system in official testing practices and the power involved in and social significance of designating some human beings as more valuable than others, and the function of such designations in denying rights and participation in governance.

A good example of this problem is evident in the properties built into IQ tests. Scoring gives the impression that IQ tests measure intelligence in the same way that rulers measure length. For example, if you ask someone how tall he or she is, they could say "I am five feet tall." Likewise, one could answer the question how smart someone is by reporting an IQ of 116. But unlike height, a magnitude inhering in or a feature of persons, the IQ metric is an artifact of how the test is constructed; intelligence quotient points do not reflect properties inhering in individuals, but rather reflect the individual's relation to society (the norm group) and social organization more generally. Note that the actual score that people are given is converted from a ranking, a percentage of how many people in their age cohort scored below them (say the eighty-sixth percentile). This percentile ranking is converted, arbitrarily, to the number 116. This gives the impression that the instrument has been used to show that an individual has 116 intelligence units in them, an impression that would not easily be created by a simple percentile score: "He has an IQ of 116." It is actually very difficult to construct a sentence with this information so that it reflects relative rank, not absolute value; such sentences are part of the daily discourse of counselors and others concerned with the management of students' school careers (see Milofsky 1989). Even with the most admirable disclaimers, this kind of talk posits a score as a property of the individual as if it were at the level of metrication, even though the score is derived based on a comparison or the presentation of a mere topology (see Schiff and Lewontin 1986).

5

The Rise of Public Education

THE IMPULSE TO MARK
ACHIEVEMENT AND ABILITY

Assessing the relative worth or value of human beings is political, since it is connected to how a social system sorts out contending claims of its members—including the claim to be a member and participate in affairs of governance. In this way, standardized tests can be examined as political theory: that which addresses itself to the origin, development, and dissolution of political power, and the justification for that power. Deciding who gets what, when, where, and how is certainly political in nature, with some commentators arguing that such decisions are the raison d'être of standardized tests (e.g., Gifford 1986). But we need to explore why and how a group's or individual's mental characteristics became relevant—even central—to how a society legitimates political rights when such characteristics had not previously been judged significant in this regard (Carson 1994).

Taking the heuristic outlined in chapter 2, the present chapter analyzes in broad terms how "struggles over standards reflect political struggles, within or between classes." This means exploring how the political aspects of the transition from a feudal to capitalist social order related to challenging the standard of hereditary right with that of merit understood as virtue and talent. Asking how "a change in standards, or who controls the standard, relate to changes in governance," leads to a discussion of the role of reason and the public in governance and the notion of "natural distinction" embedded in the theory of a "natural aristocracy." By asking the question, What is the theory of power embodied in the new standard? and how it "relates to particular social values," the specific ways in which political rights are linked to mental attributes are explored, including notions of the "equality of man" and the seemingly contradictory project of social differentiation

41

accompanying such pronouncements. The role of public schooling as a main means to institutionalize these new arrangements is given special attention.

Thus, this chapter presents in broad outline the conditions supporting the emergence of standardized testing as the standard for assessing educational endeavors. To understand standards as they exist today, we must uncover "how things got to be this way," or go to their origin. Origin refers, first and foremost, to the conditions that give rise to a thing or phenomenon. That origin can be taken to refer simply to the first time something happened constitutes a simplification of a complex analytical undertaking and therefore the notion requires some elaboration.

The first appearance of competitive written exams—the precursor to standardized tests of the present day—is found in China, some two thousand years ago (DuBois 1970). But such a location in space and time does not reveal the origin of these practices. The conditions that gave rise to competitive written exams during that historical epoch within that cultural tradition are not revealed by a date. These conditions may be similar to present conditions. To put things in a different light, when Charles Darwin spoke of the origin of species, he was not simply referring to when a biological organism first appeared as a distinct phenotype within a larger population, but the theory by which such a development generally takes place. That is, origin refers to uncovering the impetus, condition or initiation of a thing or phenomenon, and these references need not be only to one place in time. The connection to "beginning" or "first appearance" becomes relevant with the assumption of this approach: the essence of a thing or phenomenon is revealed when that thing or phenomenon first appears, and subsequently during each stage of its development—things and phenomena reveal themselves in space and time. The method derived from this presupposition is to isolate in space and time key points in the development of standardized tests for analytical treatment. This chapter thus focuses attention on the broad historical shifts that characterize the social context in which it "makes sense" to emphasize individual mental characteristics. Understanding this context is important for understanding how standardized tests functioned to institutionalize new principles of legitimate political and social practice. The following two chapters study this institutionalization process by presenting two case studies of key points in the emergence of standardized tests as the standard by which achievement and ability are determined.

Changes in classification are most effectively studied when social systems "are in the making" (Williams 1990, 5–6). Thus, the origin of standardized examinations, the basis on which educational classifications and assessments are now made, will be found in the changing conceptions of legitimate political order that accompanied the transition from a feudal to a capitalist social order. In particular, this transformation rejected a social value system based on bloodline and to a lesser extent military talent (knights). As a social system, capitalism overturned key medieval notions, rejecting that an individual's place in the social hierarchy was to be determined by relations of blood and land; the emergence of labor markets functioned to dismantle old social hierarchies and erect new ones. The emerging capitalist class targeted the notion of rule by bloodlines as particularly problematic for their efforts to establish a society governed on the basis of the sanctity of private property.[1]

Arguments against Rule by Bloodlines and for Rule by a Natural Aristocracy

Feudal arrangements established standards for legitimating who would hold political power, who had what rights and what privileges, on the basis of considerations other than mental ability or academic achievement. Hierarchical social structures and the resulting forms of vertical classification were established on the basis of family ties, military service, land holdings, and, more generally, the bonds between vassals and lords. Prior to the emergence of the modern nation-state, intellectual ability, one's level of academic achievement, and so on, were afforded relatively little space in the discourse of political thought. Where hereditary rights did not hold sway, power in Europe was established by the church; when one's ability was the basis of social position, this was mainly in the domain of the military, as nobility status was often associated with military service.

While the idea that nature had fit some humans for slavery and others for freedom—that inequality of natures produces inequality of rights—dates back to Aristotle in Western political thought, the emphasis on intellectual capacity as distinct from other physical differences of strength and beauty becomes most important in the era following the Enlightenment (Carson 1994; Dahrendorf 1968, chap. 6). With their emphasis on the mental abilities and qualities of individuals, bourgeois theorists were openly rebelling against the basic presuppositions of the feudal political order.[2] Enlightenment investigations of aristocracy challenged the entire notion of a social order legitimated on the grounds of birth, while also reducing the significance of military prowess as a standard for entry into the aristocracy. Aristocratic governments violated reason because they could too easily accommodate instability and corruption; hereditary leadership was inherently unsatisfactory because it could never ensure that individuals with the appropriate mental attributes reached positions of power (Carson 1994, 18). In this way, feudal institutions were given as failures by Enlightenment thinkers, for they were unable to produce political institutions capable of sustaining a capitalist social order.

The union of the different republics in North America that was to become the United States was being formed during a period making a break with feudal arrangements, with historic France constituting a model example of what has come to be known as feudalism, and the French Revolution the leading, albeit controversial, historical example of the West's break with this social system. Thus, Carson (1994) notes that after having toppled this feudal aristocracy, bourgeois forces faced a key problem: what is the basis for social distinction and hierarchy?

While having argued standardized tests have as their object social value, such value judgments are not unique to psychometry or the social context of its emergence. While the standard and method for marking value changed with the emergence of capitalism, the presumption and value of social hierarchies remained. Understanding the origin and function of standardized testing warrants that this postulate be elaborated. Thus we need to explore notions of reason and public and their role in liberal democracy, followed by an examination of a new means for the vertical classification of human beings. This new system postulated that mental and, in particular, academic abilities were a "natural" basis for classification and thus a means by which to identify the "natural aristocracy." This established the link between academic skill and political rights, such that this aristocracy had the right to rule over all other social groups on the grounds of its "natural" (not artificial or social) superiority. Standards used to mark the "natural aristocracy" embodied not only a theory of rights predicated on mental power, but the social outlook and views of the enlightened bourgeois reformers who created the foundation for their development.

Reason, Governance, and the Role of Public Education

In opening up his discussion on the concept of equality of education, Haney presents egalitarian thought as originating in religious doctrines and disputes. "In a sense, education was always connected with theological disputes over equality. Luther's contention that all Christians could read and interpret the Bible was, after all, predicated on a sort of equal educational capacity." As capitalist expansion and religious reformation challenged the feudal status quo, presuppositions of equality spread to secular spheres of social life. "Social philosophers," Haney continues, "began to predicate not only a common human capacity to know God's way, but also simply to reason and to know, the connection between education and equality became more explicit" (1977, 4). Reasoning, then, was no longer the purview and prerogative of the rulers and was increasingly given as an attribute of human beings as they were rendered equal both as a necessity of trade in human labor power and religious reform.

This premise of equality that accompanied religious reform and capitalist expansion enabled and coincided with the emergence of "public spheres." In their ideal form these functioned as mechanisms for the determination of authoritative bases for political action through reasoned argument. Summarizing German social theorist Habermas's study of the public sphere, Calhoun writes: "In a nutshell, a public sphere adequate to a democratic polity depends upon both the quality of discourse and quantity of participation." The "classical bourgeois public sphere of the seventeenth and eighteenth centuries was constituted around rational critical argument, in which the merits of arguments and not the identities of arguers were crucial" (1992, 2). Although originally comprised of narrow sections of European population, with little regard for the reasoning ability of, for example, women or "businesspeople," in its ideal form the public sphere was educative since "participation in argument is a means of education capable of overcoming the debilities that make some arguers inferior (and thus it is a very different matter from ascribed statuses that permanently exclude some people)." It spoke to a "general interest" sufficiently basic "that discussion about it need not be distorted by particular interests" (Calhoun 1992, 9). The *public* in the bourgeois public sphere is defined as "private individuals who join in debate of issues bearing on state authority" and thus, the public is given as a mechanism to limit or check state power over these individuals. Thus, Calhoun writes that "the public sphere was not conterminous with the state apparatus, for it included all those who might join in a discussion of the issues raised by the administration of the state. The participants in this discussion included agents of the state and private citizens" yet this public came to see itself not simply as the object of state action, but also as the "opponent of public (state) authority" (8–9). Thus, the bourgeois public sphere broke with earlier notions, postulating "a society separate from the ruler (or the state) and of a private realm separate from the public" (7).

The emergence of the bourgeois public sphere becomes an important premise of public schooling and its association with opportunity and the formation of enlightened public opinion. This was true for at least two reasons. The public sphere "helped to engender both a more widespread literacy and an approach to the printed word as a source of currently significant 'public' information." Those who thought of themselves as "the public" constituted a "certain educated elite." They were individuals who participated in the salons, coffeehouses, and other social spaces that emerged in the seventeenth and eighteenth century (Calhoun 1992, 7–9). To the degree that participation in public debate about the affairs of society is premised on the ability to argue is the degree to which such mechanisms also function to promote political equality. That social action often demanded and resulted in broader participation in this public sphere is suggestive of the importance of this sphere for formal recognition of what we now call civil rights. It is with the formation of this public sphere that we find a concrete link between political rights and mental power.

Americans followed the basic tenets of the European liberalism that grew out of these developments, resulting in the formation of modern nation-states. In this framework, expanding voting rights required expanding education. The legitimacy of political processes and institutions was to primarily rest on deliberative as opposed to coercive means, with consent of the masses favored by Enlightenment thinkers over the use of force and intimidation (Welter 1971, intro.). This was thought to be the best model for political stability and economic development.

Consent of the governed required some open discourse, debate, and investigation, with legislative bodies functioning as a space for this public debate. Such a political order must then affirm to a degree far greater than ever before the right to conscience. The economics of the need for education are fairly clear with burgeoning commerce and industry, which required both the development of science and technology and training in everything from bookkeeping to marketing. But politically, the capitalist struggle against feudalism recognized a place for the body politic or public. Liberal theories of government not only affirmed individual freedom, but service in the public interest as a general aim of government. And while this individual was narrowly conceived relative to holding property and originally limited to white men, such a conception nonetheless opened up a space for "the individual" to operate in the public sphere, independent of the whim of the king, or duty to the lord. Capitalism had to affirm individual initiative as a correlate to the aim of the private acquisition of property. Relative to the past, then, there developed an unprecedented freedom of inquiry and debate that could not be conceived during the Middle Ages, and while concern always existed about containing these freedoms, such as the fear of a "tyranny of the majority," the bourgeois revolution nonetheless established an order that out of necessity required a broadly educated populace for reasons beyond the immediate needs of the economy.

For the masses to consent, they must be able to deliberate or else the consent is empty and unconvincing. In this system, the category of the masses is given a previously unheard-of role in governance. Of course this means at a minimum that the ability to read and write beyond reference to the Bible, along with basic math and science—that is, a broader range of knowledge that could be referenced and brought to bear on matters of public concern—be broadly developed among the people: they cannot be persuaded by that which they do not comprehend.

Thus, one of the important outcomes of the fight against feudalism was the view that belief should be established on the basis of reason or argument, as opposed to blind faith or the mere utterances of authority. For belief to be established on the basis of reason, the conditions for reason itself must be created, and increasingly reformers and social theorists turned to education and the significance of educated public opinion (Welter 1962, 24–36).

The notion of educated public opinion, or enlightened public opinion, should not be narrowly dismissed as the imposition of bourgeois values, though certainly this was and is an important feature of schooling (e.g., the narrow rendering of work ethic that is fixated on producing a compliant and productive working class for the narrow benefit of the owners of the means of production). Educated public opinion assumed general education as a basis for forming opinions about the general or common interests. Education was also a means by which to keep in check public opinion so it did not lead to a "tyranny of the majority." But even if such common interests are rendered within the limits of liberal ideology—public opinion understood as that which stands against the domination of sectarian interests or a faction over all others—the public must nonetheless be exposed en masse to an elementary form of education. In fact, public education may be seen as not only educating the public but a mechanism by which it is called into being and institutionalized. The fact that common school reforms were enacted on the basis of public persuasion and not central decrees or coercion testifies to the role given educated public opinion for the establishment of legitimate government in the United States (Green 1990, 189; Welter 1962, 45–59).

These reasons are connected to a political order where the right to vote was continuously extended to more of the body politic, where public opinion was offered as the justification of government course of action or state of affairs, where members of the body politic played a formal role in the legal system as jurors—all this required that eighteenth-century notions of "widest diffusion of knowledge" be extended and given institutional forms and means of reproduction.

The prefix "public" not only refers to education controlled by the public. It also stands as an adjective describing the type of education; education geared toward the general interests. It is also literally a reference to the education of the public (or people). This is not to deny or debate that public education in the United States was greatly influenced by capitalist interests, that it was not part and parcel of state-organized racism, sexism, and so on. The issue is that part of the theory of governance of this new class—against the feudal, landed aristocracy—was the necessary production of a nonsectarian agent that could stand against rule of faction and mitigate the threat of civil war, a difficulty faced in forming a union out of republics as the *Federalist Papers* indicate (Fairfield 1961). "Only in control by the public as a whole," Cremin writes in outlining the basic principles of public education, "could the danger of *partisan control* be avoided" (1957, 19–20, emphasis added).

With these developments, then, three things stand out: (1) reasoning ability was linked to political rights when it became a basis for making claims, thus promoting a certain equality; (2) reason functioned as a new basis for legitimate political power, participation in governance, and a means to limit state power; and (3) public education became an institutional link between the public sphere and public authority, an agent mediating the interaction between "civil society" and state power.

The Natural Aristocracy:Nature as the Basis for Social Distinction

The rise of the bourgeoisie to power was accompanied by the principle of equality, yet once ascended material and political inequality still existed, and in many respects increased (Green 1990, 194–196). That the explicit precept of being created equal is supplemented with values of social difference is key to understanding the practice of public schooling in the United States. Recall that once having toppled the feudal order, the bourgeoisie confronted the dilemma of establishing a new basis for social distinction. Notably, the language of the common school—that the point is to erase artificial distinctions, while creating natural distinctions, a point we will see Horace Mann emphasized as he sought to establish new standards of achievement—is central to the writings of Thomas Jefferson on the role of education in selecting the natural aristocracy.[3] It is also noteworthy that reformers such as Horace Mann and Henry Barnard opposed private schools on the basis that they "classified society at the root 'by assorting children according to wealth, education, or outward circumstances of their parents, into different schools' and so educate 'children of the same neighborhood differently and unequally'" (Barnard quoted in Green 1990, 193).

Natural differences dominated Jefferson's consciousness to the point that a main aim of schooling was to "rake from the rubbish annually" the "best and the brightest." Understand here that the differences were not primarily individual in nature; the assumption was that individuals "naturally" fit into ranked categories or *groups*, with the natural aristocracy being the group at the apex of the social hierarchy. I am not debating that humans vary in their abilities. The point here is that Enlightenment thinkers presented reasoning ability as a natural—that is, has nothing to do with history of society—basis for the ranking of human beings so that the human group appears instead as distinct races of rulers and ruled. These distinctions are natural, but they are veiled by the "artificial" distinction of birth and class.

Thus, it is also important to understand that there was no desire to rid society of classes among major Enlightenment thinkers. Nor did these thinkers assume that all human beings possessed in equal measure all the various known human abilities. Otherwise why would one want to measure—or rather, differentiate—that which is equal at birth, unless the entire project was the establishment of a new standard of social value, of worth or merit and its antithesis? What was equal at birth was the chance to rise on the basis of one's merit. Put another way, Enlightenment thinkers were against an aristocracy by birth, but in favor of one of virtue and talent; for such an aristocracy to be legitimate, social mobility must be present, at least relative to the feudal order against which these thinkers rebelled. Mechanisms must be in place whereby individuals can rise in social status while at the same time maintaining structural inequality; individuals must be able to move between various points on the social hierarchy, but the hierarchy itself must remain.[4]

Thus, out of the need to establish a ranked social order without the presumption of a hereditary or landed aristocracy, Enlightenment thinkers looked to "nature" for justification. Recall in chapter 2 the Enlightenment drive to develop standards rooted in immutable natural phenomena, so that all may be equally subject to the standards. Just as the Earth and natural elements were the source of standards, so to in human affairs nature was the source of standards.

Because reason was the new basis for government, and this mental characteristic was generally accepted as heritable, differences in reasoning ability were given as a natural—and thus a preferred—means by which to vertically classify humankind. Because reason is given as originating in nature and not society, it transcends class lines and thus does not reflect the bias of any class. For these reasons, ordering society on the basis of mental abilities becomes egalitarian. In this way, intelligence or reasoning ability not only became an important criterion for selection, but one that is presented as "naturally" important. As Carson notes:

> Rousseau's analysis of the origin of human differences was in no way atypical of Enlightenment discussion of human nature. From midcentury mental philosophers like David Hartley or the Abbe de Condillac to late-century political writers like William Godwin, Thomas Jefferson, or even the Federalists, there was a common tendency to depict human mental and moral characteristics as somehow more fundamental, more real, and ultimately more natural than the "accidents'" of birth, wealth, or class. (1994, 17)

Indeed, the "naturalness" of categorizing human beings in terms of their mental and moral characteristics "proved a potent weapon in one of the eighteenth century's great political crusades, the dismantling of the justification for hereditary aristocracy" (Carson 1994, 17). From this presupposition emerged the happy coincidence that the property-owning class proved to be naturally superior in reason to that of the masses, and thus it was this "natural" distinction that made them fit to rule.

The degree to which the "naturalness" of this category for classifying human beings has been accepted is profoundly revealed by the struggle to extend rights. During the nineteenth century and onward, reformers advocated for the equal rights of both women and African Americans with the claim that each is equal in intellect to that of European men (Carson 1994). These arguments functioned to cement and further legitimate the linkage of mental characteristics to political rights, and as we shall see, helped create the conditions whereby educational attainment is presented as a basis for securing political rights and economic opportunities. This last point also exposes the link between the change in standard of social value and changes in the political and economic system.[5]

A letter Jefferson wrote to John Adams, dated October 28, 1813, reveals that the conception of natural aristocracy, or simply natural distinction, is in response to the premise of the equality of man that emerged with capitalism and the ideological support this conception of man received with religious reformations that postulated equality before God. Jefferson wrote:

> The selecting the best male for a Haram of well chosen females also, which Theognis seems to recommend from the example of our sheep and asses, would doubtless improve the human, as it does the brute animal, and produce a race of veritable aristoi [aristocrats]. For experience proves that the moral and physical qualities of man, whether good or evil, are transmissible in a certain degree from father to son. But I suspect that the equal rights of men will rise up against this privileged Solomon, and oblige us to continue acquiescence under the 'Amayrosis geneos aston [the degeneration of the race of men] which Theognis complains of, and to content ourselves with the accidental aristoi produced by the fortuitous concourse of breeders. For I agree with you that there is a natural aristocracy among men. The grounds of this are virtue and talents. (Jefferson 1813)

In lieu of proceeding on the basis of what would amount to eugenics, Jefferson postulates the existence of a natural (spontaneous, presocietal) aristocracy. He goes on to outline the historical basis for conceptualizing merit in terms of intelligence and character, as opposed to the feudal standard of military prowess.

> Formerly bodily powers gave place among the aristoi. But since the invention of gunpowder has armed the weak as well as the strong with missile death, bodily strength, like beauty, good humor, politeness and other accomplishments, has become but an auxiliary ground of distinction. There is also an artificial aristocracy founded on wealth and birth, without either virtue or talents; for with these it would belong to the first class. The natural aristocracy I consider as the most precious gift of nature for the instruction, the trusts, and government of society. And indeed it would have been inconsistent in creation to have formed man for the social state, and not to have provided virtue and wisdom enough to manage the concerns of the society. May we not even say that that form of government is the best which provides the most effectually for a pure selection of these natural aristoi into the offices of government? (Jefferson 1813)

Note that while Jefferson rejects the possibility of consciously breeding humans, on the grounds that it conflicts with the equal rights of man, breeding itself is not rejected (note as well that voting by an electorate is not mandated by this theory). "Worth and genius" constitute, to use a phrase in common use today, a "standard of excellence" defined by Webster's, interestingly, as "a compilation of the desired qualities and characteristics of a breed of livestock," originally, "with indication of the faults" to be especially avoided. It must be noted that such breeding signifies social value—"desired qualities and characteristics." The natural aristocracy is a distinct human breed (group), having distinct qualities that spontaneously exist within all social conditions.

Under Jefferson's plan, it was a main function of public schools to select and nurture this natural aristocracy. After elaborating his first proposal to keep at bay the artificial aristocracy—note that a main function of the natural aristocracy is to thwart tyranny by the artificial aristocracy—he reminds Adams of the second part of his plan, in which education is central.

> It was a Bill for the more general diffusion of learning. This proposed to divide every county into wards of 5. or 6. miles square, like your townships; to establish in each ward a free school for reading, writing and common arithmetic; to provide for the annual selection of the best subjects from these schools who might recieve at the public expence a higher degree of education at a

district school; and from these district schools to select a certain number of the most promising subjects to be compleated at an University, where all the useful sciences should be taught. Worth and genius would thus have been sought out from every condition of life, and compleatly prepared by education for defeating the competition of wealth and birth for public trusts. (Jefferson 1813; misspellings are in the original)

Certainly one of the most effective ways to seek out "from every condition of life" those of "worth and genius" is the competitive, written academic examination. In it resided those qualities, that "standard of excellence" deemed necessary for the government of society. It is a "natural" means of classification since performance is a reflection of the natural ability to reason. The full development of such exams was not too far off from the time Jefferson wrote the letter to Adams. By the middle of the nineteenth century, competitive academic examinations with rewards for those who succeeded were becoming increasingly widespread within Western societies (Broadfoot 1979). But these exams emerged as tools that were part of a larger project, the building of public school systems as a central feature of modern nation-states.

Public Education and State Formation

It is within this general context of the emergence of public education—that is the shift to a system of formal schooling funded and controlled by agencies of the state—that standardized testing technology is first developed in the United States. The development of public schooling as a system is an outgrowth of state building activities beginning in the nineteenth century. And while the emergence of secular state systems was part of establishing the hegemony of capitalist relations, growth in public schooling does not readily correlate with measures of capitalist expansion (Green 1990). The industrial revolution flourished in Great Britain long before it did in Prussia, for example, yet it was the Prussian and not the English model that American reformers in the mid-nineteenth century borrowed from. Britain lagged behind other nations in adopting public schools, relying through most of the nineteenth century on a patchwork of private and semipublic institutions to provide schooling for all social classes. The Netherlands organized the first successful common school system, yet would not develop significant industry until late in the nineteenth century. Public schooling was implemented considerably before the full impact of capitalist expansion was felt in Prussia and Scotland, two of the pioneers in popular education (Glenn 1988, chap. 1; Katznelson and Weir 1985, chap. 2).

This disjuncture between the level of development of industrial capitalism and the level of development of public education in the United States suggests that the link between state-formation and capitalism is not mainly in the domain of "human capital" or the development of a curriculum to train future workers. Instead, the connection is found in political responses to the social transformations brought about by early industrial capitalism in the context of a broadly accepted ideology of republicanism with an unprecedented extension of the franchise to white workingmen. "By shattering preindustrial patterns of social control that centered on the household as a unit of production," Katznelson and Weir write, "capitalist industrialization created massive new problems of order that were expressed, in part, as problems of citizenship in a republic." They continue noting that the dominant classes feared disorder, a fear Horace Mann eloquently articulated in his celebrated annual reports. These elite "articulated their concerns in terms of civic virtue, and pursued educational reform as an instrument of order. The working classes, like the working classes elsewhere, strongly desired schooling for their children. But, unlike some other working classes, they were prepared to join in political coalitions favoring public schooling because they had already been mobilized by political parties into the state as voting citizens" (1985, 45). Note that this is an excellent example of the problem of social value outlined earlier, especially as it reveals how education became linked to social status.[6] Public education was not only a central concern of workingmen's associations, it was the solution they offered to what they perceived as contemporary social problems. And Horace Mann offered the same diagnosis and solution as the workingmen little more than a decade later in his celebrated and final *Twelfth Annual Report* (see Welter 1962, 45–59, 100). Public education became a means by which workers were integrated into the state, seeing it not as an imposition of a ruling class, but instead as a "formula for citizenship," as a means by which to claim rights and counter the power of the elite (Welter 1962, 51). In this respect, schooling was given as institutionalization of this power-limiting function of the public sphere.

The extent that working people were integrated into the political process in the United States is significant. In 1750, well over 50 percent of the white male population in the Northeast already exercised a local franchise; by the time of Andrew Jackson's second election victory in 1832, property qualifications for males had been abolished in all but four states. Five states, all in the North, allotted a restrictive franchise to blacks. The taxpaying qualification was also being removed, albeit more slowly. This "represented a more broadly based suffrage than in any other country at the time. The importance of this relative extension of democratic rights on the formation of American political ideology can hardly be exaggerated" (Green 1990, 197). It is the extension of these rights that most directly correlates with the expansion of public schooling in the United States. As well, more local offices were being filled on the basis of election. The formation of political parties and their de facto rule over the political process—evidenced by the spoils system and the emergence of the "party machine"—were also an important development during the nineteenth century (Katznelson and Weir 1985, chap. 2). Much political thought of this time considered voting to have profound educational benefits and consequences in that it was a concrete expression of public opinion. Voting required "enlightened" or educated citizens who would be capable of good judgment (Green 1990, 187–208).

Almost every state in the Union, or then in the process of joining the Union, took up the question of public education at constitutional conventions, and elsewhere, during the nineteenth century. The U.S. Constitution is silent on the problem of education and it took nearly fifty years for states to seriously grapple with who was responsible for the education of the people, and what character such education should have. In 1845, education was given a special place in the Louisiana constitutional convention; in 1850, a similar situation followed in Ohio; in 1868, both South Carolina and Virginia took up the question of education in the context of constitutional conventions. In fact, most state conventions of the 1840s and 1850s provided some measures for a system of public schools (Welter 1971). It was following the so-called democratization of the Jacksonian period that the conception and role of education were codified in American thought and legislation. The expansion of popular suffrage is one important context of renewed enthusiasm for the educational requirements of democratic societies.

Differences in the development of public schooling among various Western countries are related to differences in class formation, especially the manner in which the working class related to the bourgeois state. Workingmen's associations in the United States expressed the views of a dying artisan class, not the class of wage-laborers or even skilled wage-laborers. "The workers who articulated and fought for a vision of democratic, common education were not skilled workers in the modern sense but artisans whose very existence as a class was threatened by industrialization," Katznelson and Weir contend. "The artisans who supported the common school were attracted by its *common* features, which, through democratic control and supported by mass taxation, the lack of tuition payments, and a shared curriculum across class lines, could cushion their children against social change" (1985, 20–21).

The relative strength of a given state is also important to consider. The decentralization of the U.S. system stands in stark contrast to those highly centralized systems in continental Europe, especially France. The appeal of testing as a mechanism of authority is in part rooted in a political system that gave central authorities in the United States few formal powers. And while the famous *baccalauréat* emerged in the context of the highly centralized French state under Napoleon Bonaparte, it did not emerge as an accountability mechanism. Rather, it was a mechanism of selection that served to enhance and legitimate social positions that were based primarily on wealth (Ringer 1987).

The Common School Agenda: From "Diffusion of Knowledge" to "Democratic Education"

Between the time of the founding of the United States and the middle of the nineteenth century, there occurred an important change in American political thought relative to education. While government by a "natural aristocracy" has stood as the basis for Anglo-American political thought even before the American Revolution and since, there was nonetheless a qualitative shift from an emphasis on the "widest diffusion of knowledge" promoted by Jefferson to what Welter (1962) calls "democratic education," or public schooling funded and controlled by the government, as both a means and an end of democracy.

In a letter to Joseph Cabell, Jefferson further elaborates his plan for "Ward schools," which had been proposed as one of two civil powers to be granted to the University of Virginia. Cabell had indicated to Jefferson that this provision of his bill was "likely to render the law unpopular in the country." After summarizing the voluntary nature of this plan, Jefferson counters:

> [I]f however it [the section on Ward schools] is intended that the State government shall take this business into it's own hands, and provide schools for every county, then by all means strike out this provision of our bill. I would never wish that it should be placed on a worse footing than the rest of the state. but if it is believed that these elementary schools will be better managed by the Governor & council, the Commissioners of the literary fund, or any other general authority of the government, than by the parents within each ward, it is a belief against all experience. try the principle one step further, and amend the bill so as to commit to the Governor & Council the management of all our farms, our mills, & merchants' stores. No my friend, the way to have good and safe government, is not to trust it all to one; but to divide it among the many, distributing to every one exactly the functions he is competent to. (1971, 11; verbatim from original)

Based on the English model, schooling in early America was local, voluntary, and often religiously based; and while the New England states are famous for their early legislation for common schools, nothing like a system of education overseen—let alone managed by—a central state authority existed. Education was only one of many ways to shape public behavior, and it was not given as key to social control prior to the nineteenth century. And while public monies were collected for schooling, the now-familiar distinction between public and private did not exist in either institutional or ideological form. Public monies went to privately founded schools run by teacher-entrepreneurs without any objection (Welter 1962, 9–29; see also Katznelson and Weir 1985; Reese 2007, chap. 5).

These colonial arrangements are different from what developed in the nineteenth century. Common schools that had been established in the Northeast had become neglected during the eighteenth century, a situation that Mann used to buttress his agenda (Downs 1974, 31–36). By the middle of the nineteenth century, the idea of education as a key agent of social reform, of equality, as a mechanism against the artificial aristocracy, was established as public opinion. Central to this was the idea of education as an opportunity to be provided by the government, funded through taxes, on the basis of "equal privilege for all." Jacksonian Democrats, liberal Whigs, and workingmen's associations all championed these ideas. The general thesis was that class struggle should be replaced with the struggle for education, that social distinctions are not to take place on the basis of class. Through government intervention, a system of public education would be a means by which to eradicate unnatural distinctions (Welter 1962, 45–102). Public education not only became a means to democracy, but its expression and requirement.

Horace Mann was a leading figure in what is known as the common school movement. It is within this context that essentially standardized written exams were used as tools to increase the supervisory authority of the state over schools in Boston. Mann was instrumental in bringing about many of the now-common educational arrangements such as state-run teachers colleges and libraries. Mann was also instrumental in developing the graded classroom. Although this practice is now taken for granted, the idea that students should be grouped and educated by age was revolutionary in Mann's time. In these ways, his role in promoting progressive pedagogy and curricular is second to none, all of which should be understood as part of the Whig hegemony prior to the Civil War (Downs 1974; Howe 1979; Mann [1855] 1969, 1965). As a state senator, Mann won legislation establishing the first of its kind "lunatic hospital," the building and overseeing of which Mann took an active role on behalf of the state of Massachusetts, revealing that all of Mann's efforts were informed by a broad vision for vastly increasing the role and responsibility of government in promoting the popular welfare and in this way they are part of a broad progressivism (Downs 1974, 23–27).

The idea of the common school was a particular variant of universal schooling, and while flourishing in the United States, emerged elsewhere too (see Glenn 1988). In the United States, reformers who sought to bring the schools under the state's control, including Mann, were relying on the Enlightenment notion of education as political socialization, and education as a "natural right" and "natural" basis for distinction (Mann 1847).[7] A key part of the common school ideology was that all social classes (really all whites) should be educated together so that the natural distinctions could be revealed; if classes were separated into private schools, determining natural distinction from that of social distinction would be impossible. This meritocratic logic is also evident in the age-graded classroom for which Mann was an early advocate (see Labaree 1988, chap. 3). Tyack and his colleagues describe the idea of the common school this way: "In theory the common school was to embrace all children. Indeed, a major claim made by school promoters was that if pupils of all social classes merged in the school, the rich with the poor, a shared education would begin to *erase artificial social distinctions*, while people of different backgrounds would learn to understand one another" (Tyack, James, and Benavot 1987, 16; emphasis added; see also Kaestle 1983). For Mann, improving the Boston schools was required to attract children of the rich; limiting the influence of private academies would also bolster their efforts to centralize political control over a system of tax supported education (Reese 1995, 21–52).

Mann's articulation of the political function and significance of common schools is noteworthy. "Now, surely, nothing but Universal Education [which cannot be left up to local communities and private ventures] can counter-work this tendency to the domination of capital and the servility of labor," Mann wrote in his *Twelfth Annual Report.* "If one class possesses all the wealth and the education, while the residue of society is ignorant and poor . . . the latter, in fact and in truth, will be the servile dependents and subjects of the former" (Mann 1868, 668–669). Again, this emphasizes the role given to education in opening up space for independent political participation by the masses as a means to thwart tyranny.

Arguing for a conception of equal opportunity as equal chance to acquire property, Mann continued, with the understanding that rights are affirmed by property: "But if education be *equably* diffused, it will draw property after it by the strongest of all attractions; for such a thing never did happen, and never can happen, as that an intelligent and practical body of men should be permanently poor." Note here the development of the connection between education as the development of intelligence and political rights. Mann continues: "Property and labor, in different classes, are essentially antagonistic; but property and labor, in the same class, are essentially fraternal," Mann argues. In an effort to distinguish the United States from European societies, he contends that "it is [because of] education that two thirds of the people are indebted for not being, to-day, the vassals of as severe a tyranny, in the form of capital, as the lower classes of Europe are bound to in the form of brute force." Thus, "education," he continues, "beyond all other devices of human origin, is the great equalizer of the conditions of men—the balance-wheel of the social machinery." Formal education, in this model, is the main arena for fighting for equality understood as the equal chance for natural distinction. As such, education is a political tool, for it "gives each man the independence and the means, by which he can resist the selfishness of other men." "It does better than to disarm the poor of their hostility towards the rich; it prevents being poor," this doctrine holds (669).

Public schooling thus became drawn into being a basis on which social distinctions are legitimated. It is important to understand that the eradication of social distinctions was not the aim; distinction irrespective of social class was. The spread of education, "by enlarging the cultivated class or caste," will quell class antagonisms. And Mann continues, "[I]f this education should be universal and complete, it would do more than all things else to obliterate factitious distinctions in society" (quoted in Cremin 1957, 86–87).

6

Achievement Testing
THE CASE OF HORACE MANN

This chapter focuses on what has been recognized as an important early example of systemwide accountability via standardized written examinations: Horace Mann and his evaluation of achievement in the Boston Public Schools in 1845 (Behling 1980; Caldwell and Courtis 1925; Office of Technology Assessment 1992; Resnick 1982; Ruch 1929). Boston stands as an important case because of the historically leading role Massachusetts has played in education in the United States, where its first secretary of the State Board of Education, Horace Mann, was integral not only in agitating for profound changes in Boston's schools, including changes in their evaluation, but in leading the common school movement across the country.

Educational Assessment Prior to Midcentury

The sociologist Patricia Broadfoot notes the centrality of assessment to the very existence of social life (1979, 12). Many of the social functions that are commonly attributed to tests presently in use actually predate them, in some cases by centuries or even millennia (Hoskin 1979). To appreciate the significance of the evaluation of the Boston Public Schools in 1845, it will be useful to briefly explore assessment practice in the United States up to the middle of the nineteenth century.

Prior to midcentury, teachers applied a different standard to each student. Instruction in this sense was intensely individual, as was assessment. For example, each student was required to recite different things to the teacher, thereby establishing the teacher's understanding of each student's progress. No single standard—that is, no single question or set of questions—was applied to all students. Assessment was based largely on oral presentations. Such practice made sense given the wide variation in level of education among students who also greatly differed in age.

Yet even in this context, differentiating between students on the basis of their ability was not foreign to educators. Ranking and grouping, for example, existed prior to the development of standardized testing technologies, as did "teaching to the test." The notion of "individual differences" in Western thought can be traced, in fact, all the way back to Plato. For example, instructors contended, reports Mulhern, that "it was possible to discern in the interest exhibited by the children the purpose for which God designed them," one insisting: "Does not the Voice of God, the Voice of Nature, cry aloud, Teach him the *Sanitary act of medicine*," while another manifests "an innate Love of Truth and Right, Does not this point out the profession of Law, as if a Voice from Heaven should call it out" (1933, 207). But while instructors frequently checked individual student's progress, and while they would sometimes note differences among students, there was no sense to "measure the speed of the runner" (Mulhern 1933, 140). Admitting that it is not clear to what extent students in the colonial period were grouped, Mulhern offers the case of the Penn Charter Latin School.

> In Penn Charter Latin School, the students were evidently arranged in classes, on the basis probably of achievement. Some plan of class recitation may have been small, providing great opportunity for individual instruction by the master or submaster. Differences in ability and interests of students were sometimes recognized. . . . Yet, colonial educational records are usually silent on this question, and its importance was probably not yet widely recognized. (1933, 139)

In her study of the grading systems, Smallwood affirms that colleges evaluated their students from the earliest days of their existence. She states that this is first "recognized from the earliest types of examinations. It must have been tacitly assumed that a scale of values was present whenever there were persons to be measured." The persistent custom of placing students in the position of valedictorian and salutatorian at the time of graduation is evidence that students were ranked by academic performance (1935, 41).[1]

While high schools reportedly began requiring written entrance exams during the 1820s (Reese 1995, 144), and college use of written exams was found as early as 1833 at Harvard for student recitations (Smallwood 1935, 14), until midcentury, Kandel writes, "schools and even colleges had annual 'examinations' or inspections by school 'visitors' or trustees." Those responsible for inspection were "Gentlemen of Liberal Education" and "Reverend Ministers of the Town" according to the laws of eighteenth-century Massachusetts (1936, 22). Inspectors would visit each school and question each student orally, or have the teacher do so in front of the committee. Typically a written report would follow each visit.[2] In addition to or possibly in lieu of inspections, schools and colleges sometimes relied on public displays of "disputations" and "declamations" and similar oral exercises.[3] Disputations and declamations in effect were performances. A disputation involved two persons: one disputant and one questioner. Questions and responses were worked out ahead of time, and thus the whole process relied heavily on memorization. Declamations focused on the rhetorical delivery of an oration, such as giving a speech. Emphasis on the development of skill and grace in the rhetorical arts was thus expressed through these exercises. Both of these examination methods enforced the social values of the local elite and served to hold the educational institution accountable to the local community.

Inspiring student motivation was another important function of these old, typically oral methods of examinations. Known as emulation, this method was designed to compensate for the lack of intrinsic interest in schoolwork among students by having them compete against one another for various rewards. "Nothing can contribute more to keep up a laudable Emulation and Diligence among the Youth educated in this Seminary," wrote the trustees of the Philadelphia Academy in 1770, "than regular and stated examinations of the different schools and bestowing Premiums and other marks of approbation on the most deserving scholars" (Mulhern 1933, 209). It should be noted that Horace Mann targeted this practice because he believed it dulled student moral development and sense of national unity.

From the colonial to the early national period, then, it is clear that teacher judgments and oral examinations, as well as committee inspections, were used to evaluate and sometimes rank students and hold their respective institutions accountable to the communities they served. In some cases such ranking was used to group students according to their level of learning, or as in the case of valedictorian and salutatorian to single out high achievement. Providing different curricular tracks for different groups of students was, however, yet to come, and ranked differentiation in general was not emphasized.

But by the middle of the nineteenth century, essentially standardized, competitive written exams began to be introduced in various school systems in the United States. According to the superintendent of Chicago schools, by 1857 the mode of standardized examinations, which provided the most "reliable test of qualifications, and are on the whole the most just and satisfactory to all parties," had been adopted "in nearly all the principal cities of the Union" (Kandel 1936, 27; see also Labaree 1988, 67–72; Reese 1995, 144–159).

Exams and the Struggle for the Control of Education

Literature exploring the history of testing in the United States presents the conclusion that Mann's accountability system via written exams was mainly driven by concerns for efficiency. The role of these new exams in bringing local schools under the supervisory authority of the state is minimized and/or rendered unintended. In turn, this posits little role for standardized testing technology in state formation.[4]

Leading testing experts have argued that changes in "assessment technology over the last two centuries . . . were all geared toward increasing efficiency and making the assessment system more manageable, standardized, easily administered, objective, reliable, comparable, and inexpensive, particularly as the numbers of examinees increased" (e.g., Madaus and O'Dwyer 1999, 689). Haney and Madaus present a similar view when speaking about Horace Mann and his Boston School Committee: "In the nineteenth century . . . written exams were instituted in high schools in Boston because visiting committees did not have enough time to hear the recitations and performances of the increasing numbers of students" (1989, 685).

While it would be one-sided to ignore concerns for efficiency in establishing standardized testing technology as the standard for assessing educational institutions, it is doubtful that standardized tests have their origin in lack of efficiency. Note, for example, that Mann thanks the Examining Committees for the "labor and care expended in reducing the results of this [new] examination to tabular form" (quoted in Caldwell and Courtis, 1925, 273). This suggests that labor time in and of itself is not the issue. That Britain, until very recently, used a system of inspectors as the main mechanism of accountability shows that standardized written examinations were one of several possible arrangements (Wilson 1996).

Equally if not more important, however, is this: rendering written exams as efficient and objective is merely a claim to accurately describe social reality in functionalist terms. But why were these particular notions of objectivity and efficiency chosen to justify the new exams when they had previously not been important? Note, for example, that by the 1820s a large percentage of school-aged children were enrolled in some kind of school, at least in the older sections of the northern United States (Tyack, James, and Benavot 1987, 26). From this it might be argued that it was not the "numbers of examinees" alone that initiated the demand for standardized written exams. The drive to build a public school system that shifted responsibility for education from the family, church, and community to the state is more likely the decisive factor influencing the rise of standardized testing.[5] During the colonial and early national period, formal education beyond basic literacy was reserved for a few select white men who would work within the church or government. By midcentury, as evidenced by the development of the high school and its dual curriculum, formal schooling beyond literacy not only trained leaders of church and state, but those who would work in the growing professions associated with the rise of industrial capitalism. The change from oral to written standardized exams occurred as formal education increasingly became government controlled and funded, with the attending common school ideology that all citizens were to attend schools together, measured against a common standard adopted by the state. Not only did this promote a fair means for choosing the "best and brightest" from among the white, Anglo-Saxon population, but it also reframed education as an endeavor of the state government. While written exams made dealing with larger numbers of students less unwieldy, it is the notion of mass, or popular, education in its political aspects, not simply in terms of administrative logistics, that should be emphasized. The new exams and the graded school system they supported reflected as much the change in the aim of education as it did in the corollary that this meant more students would be attending schools for longer periods of time. Such a system was necessary, in fact, for American meritocratic ideology and practice (Labaree 1988).

The son of a minister, Horace Mann was both a successful lawyer and a politician, occupying leading positions in the state government of Massachusetts. Based on his advocacy of using state power for public works, Edmund Dwight, a like-minded wealthy financier, fellow Whig and Unitarian, suggested to Mann the position of secretary for the new Board of Education.[6] Mann struggled over whether to take the position, noting its importance as well as its uncertainties; Dwight's insistence appears to have played a key role in pushing Mann towards acceptance (Cremin 1957, intro.).

Virtually the only power that Mann and the board were granted by state law was that of requiring annual school returns of statistics and other information, including that produced by tests. Information, and his interpretation of it, was Mann's main weapon in fighting what he consistently referred to as ignorance and sectarianism. Foreshadowing the present reliance on information to support reform, Mann effectively used this power to collect evidence to buttress his ideas. "Mann's requests for information, and use of the information he received," writes Glenn, "were in some respects the key elements of his influence over the development of the common school" (1988, 123). While some of "the information was fairly obvious, such as the enrollment of schools and the number of days they were in operation" Mann used these reports "to show how much needed to be done to improve the schools and, as the years went by, how much he had accomplished" (ibid.).

Caldwell and Courtis suggest that a direct impetus for the development of the new type of exam came from the debate that had been raging between Horace Mann and the Boston schoolmasters (see Katz 1968). In his *Seventh Annual Report*, Mann reported in an unfavorable light the condition of the Boston schools, sparking the debate.

> It was disturbing to the people of Boston to have their costly schools attacked by a public official and compared unfavorably with schools in Germany and other foreign countries. When the time came for annual inspection of the common schools, as the grade schools were called, they determined that the occasion called for something more thoroughgoing than the conventional inspection. No direct reference was made in the Survey Report itself to the controversy which had been carried on during the three years previous, yet it is easy to read between the lines. (see Caldwell and Courtis 1925, 5)

In discussing the first achievement test that the Boston Committee developed under Mann's tutelage, Resnick writes:

> Although the tests showed that there were deficiencies of instruction, and perhaps excessive difficulty of the curriculum, the results seem not intended primarily as helpful advice for teachers. The most important reported result, an *unintended* one from the standpoint of the school committee, was to make city teachers and principals accountable to supervisory authority at the state level. (1982, 180; emphasis added)

Yet Caldwell and Courtis suggest that it could have been Mann himself who thought of the new standardized exams, and thus was aware of their administrative benefits. If Mann himself did not conjure up the idea, the other likely source is within the Grammar School Committee, for the Writing School Committee produced a much less thorough report, and prepared less satisfactory tests than the Grammar School Committee (1925, 25).

Were the results of the committee's actions "unintended" by those on the committee? There is evidence to the contrary. Samuel G. Howe was one of three members of the Grammar School Committee to inspect such schools, the same committee that developed the new-type tests; in fact, Howe was the author of the report so adored by Mann. The committee proposed "in addition to the usual mode of oral examination, [a] plan of submitting to the scholars a series of printed questions on all the subjects studied in the schools" (Caldwell and Courtis, 1925, 6). Howe was not only a close friend of Mann. Mann organized Howe to be on the School Committee. After the controversy had erupted with the Boston schoolmasters regarding Mann's Prussian-influenced reform agenda, Schultz writes:

> Close friends and other leading citizens of Boston jumped to Mann's defense. Mann himself launched caustic counter-attacks, in the vindictive hope that "thirty one of them hung on the same shaft would look like a string of onions." Following public and private charges and counter-charges, Mann and his friends decided to bore from within the system itself. In the fall of 1844 Mann encouraged his close friend Samuel Gridley Howe to seek the election of himself and others of like mind to the School Committee. In this way, they might gain the upper hand in properly administering the schools. (1973, 139)

During the December caucus of the Whig Party, Schultz cites an observer who said "Howe had packed the hall with citizens friendly to Mann." Howe secured, through various activities, the nomination of at least six other reform-minded candidates; while not all six were elected, Howe was victorious. "Enough men took their places on the School Committee to promise that Horace Mann's demands for centralization of authority in overseeing the schools would have a sympathetic following" 1973, 139–140).

Documenting Failure

In his *Common School Journal*, Horace Mann reprinted "copious extractions from the late Reports of the Annual Examining Committees of the Boston Grammar and Writing Schools" in which he offered an explicit and elaborate justification for standardized written exams, and more generally, his vision of education (Caldwell and Courtis 1925, 237).[7] Developed under the leadership of his ally Howe, this new practice presented portions of the student body in the Boston schools with the same written questions, under similar conditions, graded according to a single rubric. "In no instance before," Mann exclaimed, "have these schools ever been subjected to a thorough, scrutinizing examination, and to such an examination as would make their condition known to the public, as well as the committee" (ibid.). In extolling the virtues of the new exam, Mann presented his educational theory, with the exam results serving to affirm what Mann had been asserting for years. Evidence now existed in "black and white" for the "common eye" to see. Foreshadowing the rhetoric of today's reformers, Mann emphasized that, "by far the largest item in this [state's] expenditure is for the Grammar and Writing Schools" (ibid., 246), yet exam results suggested little return for such a large investment. The schools were in dire straits, according to the new exams, producing failure in unheard-of numbers. Students could not spell, write complete sentences, or even conceptualize that water can run northward.

These results are not surprising considering the difficulty of the existing curriculum and exam questions given to prepubescent youth.[8] But the level of difficulty of the new exam is not the only issue. These written exams represented a new standard, with an emphasis that reflected the educational goals of Mann and like-minded reformers, and not the goals and methods adopted by Boston's educators.

For example, Mann attributes some of the failure to the organization of the school, notably that the school had two heads. This, he said, was related to the unnatural division of the curriculum as well as the problem of who should ultimately be held accountable for failure. By having a grammar department and writing department the masters were, according to Mann, trying to cultivate the same tree in two different gardens. "Many of the studies are so connected together that they cannot be torn asunder without fatal injury to each." For example, the organization of chirography and English grammar under different masters explains students' "illegible and disgraceful scrawls" and for Mann suggests that "the kindred exercises in handwriting and in written language had not been properly combined in one exercise." Further, if the facts point to a deficient teacher, Mann asks, what is to be done if there are two teachers, "how can responsibility be fastened upon either"? "No navies sail with two admirals; no armies march with two commanders. When Rome tried this, she lost the battle of Cannae" (Caldwell and Courtis 1925, 249–253). Note that such an organizational structure does not enable centralized, state control.

Targeting teachers, Mann emphasized that the new tests made known, "with inevitable accuracy, the motive-powers by which [students] have been governed; for, other things being equal, the proficiency made by pupils will always be greater or less, according to the elevated or the degrading character of the motives by which they are governed, and incited to study" (Caldwell and Courtis 1925, 237). Exam results pointed to the negative impact of inducing student diligence in study and adherence to the authority of the masters via competitions for prizes. To reformers, this "emulation" was "the commencement of that competition,—that feverish aspiration for office and place,—which we see in after-life going on all around us, and which makes the eye of enlightened humanity weep." Moreover, emulation constituted "a desire to excel for the *sake of the gratification of being superior to others.*" Recitation from a book "is not teaching." Teaching, Mann said, is "Exposition of the principles contained in the book; showing its connection with life, with action, with duty" (Caldwell and Courtis 1925, 241).

These criticisms reflect a belief that public schools should be the main institution to socialize and unify students, enable them to reason and thus participate in civic life. These efforts to establish public agents for the formation of a united citizenry echo Whig concerns regarding corruption and place-seeking, about national and social unity more generally, and their belief that education is a bulwark for political stability (Howe 1979).

Again targeting teachers, Mann wrote that "this method of examination tests, in a most admirable manner, the competency or sufficiency of the teaching which the pupils have received." And he further explains, "If the scholars fail to answer" questions whose solution can be directly found in the texts used, the students "must bear a portion at least of the dishonor." "But," he continues, "if they answer from the book accurately and readily, but fail in those cases which involve relations and applications of principles, the dishonor must settle upon the heads of the teachers" (Caldwell and Courtis 1925, 242–244).

The public presentation of the exam results in the *Common School Journal* emphasizes their role in forming public opinion. It is clear that this information was used as a weapon against the Boston schoolmasters who had been resisting state-initiated reform efforts. It is also the case that Mann's report aimed to discredit the schoolmasters in an effort to justify the state's right and ability to enter into educational supervision.

Political Theory and the Justification for the New Standard

The changes in assessment that Mann help engender were premised on the new republican theory of rule by a "natural aristocracy" and a theory of opportunity that went well beyond the notion of "diffusion of knowledge" that guided earlier public school efforts. In this newer model, the state was to actively take responsibility for the common good. Like the newly formed nation-state, written competitive examinations were neutral, standing above politics or special interests. With all of these basic premises—ones of political theory and not educational psychology or administration—the foundation of standardized tests for the expansion of state power was set.

Although Mann did not use the word *standardization*—for it had not yet come into being—the argument he gave in asserting the merits of the new written exams are the same generally given for standardized tests. Caldwell and Courtis concurred with Mann's assessment of the report's historic significance, arguing that the committee's work constituted the first scientific attempt to measure educational achievement, noting that it took fifty years for Mann's precedent to be fully realized (1925, 7).

In support of the new method of examination, Mann cites seven reasons for adopting the new method. Kandel's summation is helpful. He writes, quoting Mann appropriately:

(1) This method is impartial, since the same questions are set to all pupils in the same class in all schools. "Scholars in the same school, therefore, can be equitably compared with each other; and all the different schools are subjected to measurement by the same standard." Further, the questions in a written examination as contrasted with those in an oral examination are equal in ease or difficulty. (2) The new method is far more just than any other to the pupils themselves. In an oral examination of a whole class each pupil is questioned for at most two minutes; while in the written test he has a whole hour in which to arrange his ideas. (3) Accordingly the method under consideration is the most thorough, since pupils are not subjected to the chance of the few questions that can be given in the brief time of an oral examination but have a wider range suited to a greater range of attainment and ability. (4) The written examination does not, like the oral examination, give the teacher an opportunity to interrupt the procedure or offer suggestions to the pupils. (5) It removes all possibility of favoritism. (6) It determines, beyond appeal or gainsaying, whether pupils have been faithfully and competently taught, for while the oral question tends to call for a factual answer, in the written examination the pupils are able to develop ideas and show the connections of facts. (7) Finally in a written examination "a transcript, a Daguerreotype likeness, as it were, of the state and conditions of the pupils' minds, is taken and carried away for general inspections"; that is, a permanent record is available by which schools may be compared with each other or each school may measure its own progress. (1936, 26)

By arguing that standardized written exam procedures create the condition for fair or "equitable" comparisons, Mann establishes a mainstay of present testing efforts: without a common standard, the relative performance of students and schools cannot be fairly ascertained. In particular, this new method facilitated the age-graded classroom, a reform introduced by Mann and key for the functioning of educational opportunity via achievement, or meritocracy.

It also, importantly, establishes a basis for state power as an arbiter that is above special interests. By establishing a common standard for comparison, Mann helped bring all those measured by that standard into a single system supervised by a central authority. While educators were always conscious of their "rivalries"—colleges were always curious about

their counterpart's standards (Smallwood 1935)—it was now the state
that established a standard for comparison of schools. It was the power
to set standards, and thus the basis for judgment, that was being usurped
from the local schoolmasters. In this way, the establishment of standardized written exams as equitable methods of comparison was about expanding state power.

This new standard also reflected the political ideology that presents
the state as a neutral body that stands above conflicts and acts to sort
them out according to established norms of justice. The notion of impartial or "neutral" is very prominent in the thinking of the nineteenth-century reformers and assumed that the values propagated by the cultural
elite through public education were neutral, nonsectarian, and indeed obvious to any reasonable person (Glenn 1988). Historiography of this period is clear that the common school was premised on being nonpartisan
and nonsectarian. This ideology surfaced repeatedly in state constitutional
debates and educational provisions, in the speeches of politicians and
school leaders, and in the textbooks children read in school (e.g., Kaestle
1983; Tyack, James, and Benavot 1987).

In fact, one reason Mann favored the new method is that committeemen had been charged with putting difficult questions to the child of
an adversary or easy ones to a friend's children (Caldwell and Courtis
1925, 242; Reese 1995, 147). Likewise, and again clearly targeting teacher
authority, the new exams also eliminated the "officious interference of
the teacher." Exams were objective because their results, as well as their
difficulty, were in "black and white" and thus constituted a permanent
record that could be viewed by everyone, for "general inspection" (Caldwell and Courtis 1925, 242–243).

With these charges Mann targeted the legitimacy of organization and
administration of the schools. Standardizing assessment would solve this
legitimacy problem, according to Mann. Put another way, by limiting the
power of the local schoolman to construct the form and content of the examinations, the state limited conflicts over matters of academic assessment
and set a precedent where it would stand in place of the teacher as the judge.

Of course, this claim to neutrality has its limits. If this new exam is
"impartiality itself," as Mann described it, then the question of who sets
the standard cannot be posed—it simply appears as rational or natural to
any thinking person. It claims, as the future metric system would, to be established on the basis of nature, which all were equally subject to. Interestingly, Mann writes:

> It is true that the committees, from year to year, under the old
> method, may make known their opinion,—they may write it out
> and publish it;—but different committees will have different

standards of excellence; and thus it is quite possible that a school may have a brightening reputation, while in reality it is running down, and a waning one while it is improving. If every man's foot is to be taken as twelve inches long, it becomes an important question by whose foot we shall measure. So of the different standards of judging in the minds of different men. (quoted in Caldwell and Courtis 1925, 243; punctuation in original)

Thus the problem of who sets the standard is raised, both in practical terms as well as in terms of legitimacy. But Mann does not recognize this as a question for his new test. "Whose foot" is Mann's test based on? What interests does it represent? It was, as the Boston schoolmasters knew, far from a neutral endeavor and instead reflected the particular interests and outlook of the then-dominant Whig faction in American government (see Howe 1979).

In chapter 2 it was noted that "just measures" are often taken as symbols of justice in general, and that practices "bound up with man's attitude to measurement assume the character of a symbolic expression of many elements of popular 'social philosophy'" (Kula 1986, 9). Strikingly, Mann commends the new exams for being "fair to all" or "giving the same advantage to all," and specifically states that, as far as the exam is concerned, "all are born free and equal" (Caldwell and Courtis 1925, 239), clearly establishing a link between the new method of examinations and the key components of the ideology underpinning the establishment of the new republic. Here Mann has taken the notion of political equality and applied it to the sphere of education, giving educational institutions an unprecedented role in social reproduction. This not only reveals that education is tightly integrated into a political practice based on a theory of democracy, but that standard-setting is undertaken by the state itself based on the precepts of the newly framed Constitution. This was not the standard teachers were applying to their students before Mann and his reformers went into action. From the point of view of the new republic, the old system failed because it could not meet the demands of the new nation in social, political, or economic terms.

Mann also showed a great deal of technical foresight with respect to some of the assumptions and practices common to present-day standardized tests. For example, Mann articulates psychometric notions of "reliability" when he argues that "[e]ach question is a partial test, and the greater the number of questions, therefore, the nearer does the test approach to completeness" (Caldwell and Courtis 1925, 239). Mann also seemed keenly aware of the importance of sampling when he argued:

To give out two or three questions on the whole subject of grammar, or geography, for instance, or to require the solution of a single question in arithmetic, resembles not a little the device of that Scholastikos in the fable, who, wishing to sell his house, carried a brick to market as a specimen. It is true the brick gave some indication about the house, as a single answer may do about a pupil's knowledge of a study; but both a discreet purchaser and a discreet examiner would like some additional information. (Caldwell and Courtis 1925, 240)

Thus, the exams determined whether pupils had been taught, "beyond appeal or gainsaying." Importantly, Mann connects the general notion of reliability with justice. The theory is that more questions and more time for each student to answer them is more just because it increases the opportunity for a student to show what he or she has learned. Thus, the sampling principle of psychometry can be understood as an opportunity theory: the more items on the test, the more the true value of the individual is assessed, and hence the more opportunity for fair judgment.

Mann also asserted that items on the test should be based on the curriculum taught. This was explicitly the case with the spelling items.

To test the knowledge of the children in regard to what they had read, the committee selected twenty-eight words,—not from the dictionary, nor from books with whose contents the children were not familiar, but from the reading books used in their own schools, from books which many of them had read for years, and part of which they had committed to memory. (Caldwell and Courtis 1925, 260)

Taking all this into account, Mann's arguments foreshadowed the psychometric principle of there being a relationship between the validity of an assessment and its reliability. A test is more reliable and valid the more it samples a specific domain related to the "construct" being assessed. Mann also thought it important to make the items on the test get progressively more difficult, that the test be "suited to a greater range of attainment and ability."

Summary

There are several things that should be emphasized. The first is the general analysis that the function of assessment did not fundamentally change. In particular, I showed that ranking student achievement, differentiating between various abilities, and the use of standards in doing so occurred before Mann's new exam, although relative to today, these early efforts were modest at best. As well, while accountability was argued to be a general feature of any assessment system, significant was the transference of accountability from local communities to the state. This process was shown to be conscious, and not accidental as has been suggested by some historians. What changed then was the particular nature of the standard of assessment and the organization of accountability. It is the standard of judgment, and not the functions of assessment in general that changed.

The new standard represents an increase in (1) emphasis on the differentiation of students based on (2) a common standard, hence increased standardization. Individualized schooling could never function to serve a project of promoting equal opportunity via impartial comparisons of academic performance. Increased differentiation, and the application of the same standard to a given population, also suggests changes in values. So, for example, writing was increasing in value with Mann's new tests. The capacity to apply principles, to reason, was to be valued over memorization; enticing students to learn was to replace the methods of emulation and corporal punishment. In fact, Mann made an important link between the outputs of the school and the methods applied in the school—memorization without the ability to reason was the outcome of the use of the methods of emulation and corporal punishment. It is the increased power of differentiation that suggests the increased significance of these qualities being assessed. As well, standardization itself was given as a neutral value. Without it, assessment would be illegitimate. Remember that the broad definition of standardization simply refers to fair competition. Mann argued that it was illegitimate to have assessments of various schools with different means of judgment; such would be invalid, unfair, and unjust. The aforementioned qualities signify the standard's content.

Many of these desired changes were reflected in the new tests. The tests constituted what was desired and what was not desired, Mann's "standard of excellence." Thus, in an address to teachers, Mann suggests that each ask themselves the following question: "Have I a clear, distinct, living conception of what a man, formed in the image of God, should be; of the various excellences, he should possess; of the innumerable vices and weaknesses, from which he should be free" (Mann 1965, 140). But for this question to be answered in a good way, from the perspective of Mann, a common standard was needed, one that embodied the pedagogy, curriculum, and school organization he and the Whig faction he served valued.

7

Intelligence Testing
THE CASE OF ALFRED BINET

The main role of the academic achievement test adopted by Horace Mann was to increase supervisory authority of the state. While the new exams functioned to make public education more accountable to a central state authority, it also served as an instantiation of reformers' educational philosophy. This chapter explores Alfred Binet's new standard of intelligence as it emerged in the context of the secularization of education in France. As was the case with Mann, Binet's standard served as a means to further legitimate state control over education. The emergence of this standard is linked to secular governing principles derived from the new social sciences.

As was the case with the early Boston achievement test, this chapter offers a different interpretation of an otherwise well-worn topic in educational history, namely, the work of Alfred Binet. Existing historiography around Binet blocks a critical analysis of his new standard for intelligence and the aim for which it was developed. The emphasis on contrasting the humanist-sounding orientation of Binet with the overt racism of his American counterparts has allowed for the maintenance of the prevailing standard of intelligence, where emphasis is placed on different interpretations of what the "scores mean." But this chapter will show that Binet's standard of intelligence was initiated in the context of definite power struggles over the structure and function of education. Supporters sought tools such as the intelligence test to institute new governing arrangements. As was the case with Mann, supporters' concerns for social stability and unity were evident in the adoption of what would become IQ.

This phase of the study begins by exploring the shift in the meaning and practice of the notion of equality of educational opportunity that occurred with a change in focus on achievement in the nineteenth century to a focus on ability at the beginning of the twentieth century.

From Achievement to Ability

From the time of the early national period to the beginning of the twentieth century, a shift in emphasis from academic achievement to academic ability occurs in both France and the United States. It must be understood that a change in emphasis is at issue; achievement testing has never ceased to be of concern.

Chapter 3 suggested that achievement tests point to what constitutes achievement, success, and thus the desired "output." Ability testing is concerned with who has what ability, and thus the question of what type of education individuals of differing abilities should receive is posed. The particular change here is a move from assessing what had been learned, to what an individual should learn in the future—that is, from what constituted being successful to who would be successful at what; not merely what success is, but what is needed for success. By virtue of their greater intelligence, academically successful students would receive an education consistent with the increasingly important role of the "expert" and "scientific" management of society. This change of course materialized in the form of a differentiated curriculum in addition to establishing special education as a field.

Yet, an argument can be made that the distinction between tests of ability and achievement are tenuous. Without knowing the name attached to a given test, it is sometimes difficult to determine whether that test is intended to measure an individual's academic ability or his or her academic achievement. Many ability tests contain similar items to those of achievement tests, and vice versa. This gives rise to commentators focusing on the use of the test: is it to determine what has been learned or what can be learned; for example, IQ-type tests have been used to assess the effectiveness of educational programs.[1] But this distinction represents, in fact, a pivotal theoretical development, one latent up to this point, but with Binet's work it takes center stage. With this development a more complete theory developed whereby achievement is explained by ability. This change occurred as more and more of the populace had increasing access to education at all levels.

This theoretical shift represents a change in the theory of equal opportunity. During the time of Mann, emphasis was placed on providing all the Anglo-American youth of an area the same free public education. All the youth were to be educated together, in like manner, inculcating in them equally the republican values deemed so important by Protestant reformers. Binet argues against this approach, noting that some students could not benefit from the then-typical academic, classical education. Students identified as intellectually weak should be provided with different educational opportunities (see Yerkes 1987). Latent in this view is the idea that equal opportunity means being prepared for one's future role in society, not fair competition for social positions (Coleman 1977; Kliebard 1986). And it was the testing expert who was to decide a student's future, a decision that is in constant need of justifying.

From Medical to Psychological Methods

Binet's work marks a break with then-traditional methods of measuring intelligence. The impulse to measure intelligence was alive well before Binet's test of intelligence and, for example, can be seen in the work of Francis Galton and Paul Broca. The main problem with these earlier efforts is that they were not yielding the expected results. Based on the precepts of British empiricism, it was reasoned by Galton that those with the fastest reaction time would have the highest intelligence. With this approach, physical attributes and capacities were the standard for measuring intelligence. "Galton had built such a test," Schiff and Lewontin point out, but when "he found out that the man-in-the-street could do as well on his test as people that he considered *a priori* as more intelligent, he finally gave it up. This is not surprising considering Galton's ethnocentric view of human intelligence" (1986, 21). By 1901, James McKeen Cattell had established that there was no relationship between sensory discrimination and indices of intellectual performance. Originally basing his study of intelligence on the work of Broca, Binet came to a similar conclusion: students' head size did not correlate with teachers' ratings of student intelligence (Gould 1981, 147). The significant change with the work of Binet and Théodore Simon rests with the development of the psychological method of examination: it was the thoughts and mental processes of individuals that were the target. This method allowed for a measure for intelligence that did correspond to a priori notions of various individuals' place within the social organization of society.

The Need to Reexamine Binet's Work

Determining pivotal points in history is difficult. There is always the possibility of forcing history to fit a preconceived model. It is precisely because of the received wisdom regarding Binet that an argument can be made that the massive campaign to test the intelligence of U.S. Army recruits reveals the essence of IQ theory and practice as it was applied in the United States, and thus it should stand as a pivotal point in history (e.g., Baker 1990). But such an argument assumes that there is a fundamental difference between the work of the originators of the IQ method and those who applied this method in the United States—notably, Lewis Terman and Robert Yerkes (Chapman 1988). This line of thinking gives a great deal of emphasis to the differing views of the test's inventor and its adherents in the United States concerning the heritability of intelligence (Haney 1984). Explicitly and implicitly, much of the discussion emphasizes the apparent humanism of Binet, contrasting it with the profoundly racist views of Terman et al. Simply knowing that Binet said more humane-sounding things than Terman, for example, does not prove in any way that the test Binet and Simon invented and the test Terman further developed are essentially different in either theory or practice.

Such an analysis, in any case, would likely lead to an investigation of the circumstances surrounding the army tests as a distinct path from that initiated by Binet. It is certainly true that the army's use of the new tests was a very important development (Haney 1984). But historiography appears to miss the fact that Binet and Simon first advocated the utility of their test of intelligence for improving social organization:

> Let us point out the very great utility to humanity that would result from giving the intellectual test to young recruits before enlisting them. Many morons, that is to say, young men who on account of their weak minds are unable to learn and understand the theory and drill of arms and to submit to a regular discipline, come to the medical examination, and are pronounced "good for military service," because one does not know how to examine them from the intellectual point of view (Binet and Simon 1916, 272).

In this concluding section of their text, Binet and Simon elaborated various uses of their new test, not only in education, but also in the courts as well as the military. Something fundamental might be missed if the original development of the intelligence test is not reinvestigated.

The Irrelevance of the Nature-Nurture Debate for IQ Theory

Binet's theory did not focus on answering the nature-nurture question. Further, the nature-nurture debate itself appears to have obscured the nature and origin of Binet's test. To explore this it will be useful to examine Binet and Simon's views on the stability of intelligence, their approach to and concern with its etiology, and group differences in intelligence more generally.

Binet and Simon viewed intelligence (as distinct from mental level) to be stable. Evidence of this can be found in their discussion about changes in the classification of an individual's intelligence. "No doubt," they write, "it is possible—perhaps even probable that a child who at five years has scarcely the intellectual level of a child of two, will be the same at ten or fifteen years" (1916, 143). In discussing the 1908 version of their new scale, they write: "It is understood that these diagnoses apply only to that present moment. One who is an imbecile today, may by the progress of age become a moron, or on the contrary remain an imbecile all his life. One knows nothing of that; the prognosis is reserved" (270). The changes in intelligence considered possible are not significant from the social point of view (one would be comforted little by the promotion from imbecile to moron). While they did believe intelligence could be developed through instruction, it does not follow that they did not conceive of intelligence to be a stable feature of individuals. The project of classifying those who will not do well in "normal" school—their stated objective—presupposes that intelligence is relatively stable. Without this assumption, classification would be impossible.

At the same time, however, Binet and Simon are consistently agnostic, even uninterested, as to the nature of this consistency. They write:

> We have nothing to do either with his past history or with his future; consequently, we shall neglect his etiology, and we shall make no attempt to distinguish between acquired and congenital idiocy; for a stronger reason we shall set aside all considerations of pathological anatomy which might explain his intellectual deficiency. (1916, 37)

Although it is strange for psychologists to say they have nothing to do with the future of a student whose educational opportunity rests in part on the results of their evaluation, it is clear that the test was developed irrespective of etiology. And while assuming the position that intelligence is a relatively stable trait of an individual, they also assume the position that their test does not shed light on the origin of measured intelligence or intellectual level (1916, 143–144).

Throughout their writings, Binet and Simon do distinguish between "natural" and "cultured" intelligence, yet they never set out to insist on the primacy of either. By the 1908 revision, Binet and Simon concluded the following regarding what it was that their scale actually measured.

> We do not measure the intelligence considered separately from a number of concrete circumstances—the intelligence which is needed for understanding, for being attentive, for judging. It is something far more complex that we measure. The result depends: first, on the intelligence pure and simple; second, on extra scholastic acquisition capable of being gained precociously; third, on scholastic acquisition made at a fixed date; fourth, on

acquisitions relative to language and vocabulary, which are at
once scholastic and extra–scholastic, depending partly on the
school and partly on the family circumstances. (1916, 259)

Binet and Simon thus developed a new standard that included both
natural and social aspects; it was not significant to make claims about their
relative importance. Nonetheless, they did consistently give intelligence as
a faculty (never completely breaking with faculty psychology). Far from
simply constructing a scale to rank the mental level of students, Binet and
Simon constructed a theory where various faculties—intelligence, scholastic ability—were the cause of behavior. Binet and Simon began their work,
in fact, with the understanding that a student could not benefit from regular instruction, "because of the state of his intelligence" (1916, 9).

Here lies the reason for Binet and Simon's contradictory position regarding the measurement of intelligence. On the one hand, they consistently
refer to their scale as a measurement of the property intelligence. Yet, Binet
and Simon were clear that their scale is not a form of measurement:

The scale properly speaking does not permit the measure of the intelligence, because intellectual qualities are not superposable, and
therefore cannot be measured as linear surfaces are measured, but
are on the contrary, a classification, a hierarchy among diverse intelligences; and for the necessities of *practice* this classification is
equivalent to a measure. (1916, 41; emphasis added) [2]

"On the contrary," Nash exclaims. A classification by level of performance would have served most adequately. "It was not the necessities of
practice but the necessities of theory that led Binet to announce his invention of a 'metric scale of intelligence.'" Had Binet admitted that children
were merely classified by level of performance or by level of mental development, there would have been no basis on which to account for school
attainment in terms of measured functional intelligence (1990, 15–16).

Binet and Simon's assumption that lack of intelligence stood behind
school failure is possibly quite significant when viewed in light of the present context emphasizing that "all children can learn." Possibilities other
than a weak intellect could explain endemic failure to advance from grade
to grade such as an irrelevant and limited curriculum, poor teaching, or the
impact of poverty. Perhaps significant numbers of those attending French
schools at the end of the nineteenth century were not native French speakers, whose instruction was, nonetheless, in French (Weber 1976, 204–338).

Despite their repeated claims to be only concerned with practical
matters, Binet and Simon were responding to theoretical as well as practical demands: it was the needs of theory that required them to insist

their instrument allowed for the measurement of intelligence. With this orientation, it is possible to see the emphasis on measuring a property of individuals as directed toward justifying differential education, a problem the French government was intending to address (1916, 9).

Thus if one looks at it from the point of view of the theory itself, the significance lies not in any assumption about how the laws of genetics impact the development of human intelligence. Rather, significance rests with how the theory postulates intelligence to be a property of individuals in such a way as to correlate with prevailing social arrangements. The nature-nurture debate obscures what is most significant about the development of IQ theory, the core of which is evident in both environmentalist as well as hereditarian interpretations of scores—groups differ in intelligence even though the majority of variance in IQ scores is within, not between, groups. The theory works irrespective of cause. Validation of the theory rests, in fact, on the degree to which the results of the assessment correspond to prevailing forms of social differentiation. That is, the property that is explicitly theorized to inhere in the individual is implicitly theorized as a property concerning the individual's relationship to society (hence the inclusion of "natural" and "cultured" intelligence in the scale). With this understanding it is possible to make sense of Binet's thinking on intelligence tests as group differentiation. That is, the goal was to group children as intelligent and unintelligent, and to grade (value) the various levels of the unintelligent (also see Wolf 1973, 152–154). From the point of view of this goal, it mattered little whether such differences were primarily biological or environmental in origin. The genius of the theory rests in how it postulates one group as "naturally" superior to the other without the assumptions of biology, for reason had already been established as a natural basis for distinction, irrespective of the origin of differences in reasoning ability.

Such grouping, as Binet and Simon were well aware, corresponded with social class (1916, 316–329). Arguing for the significance of their test of intelligence, Binet and Simon write:

Of what use is the measure of intelligence? Without doubt one could conceive many possible applications of the process, in dreaming of a future where the social sphere would be better organized than ours; where everyone would work according to his known aptitudes in such a way that no particle of psychic force should be lost for society. That would be the ideal city. (1916, 262)

This is a vision of a social class system organized along the lines of intelligence, in essence no different from the aim of the American testing movement. But Binet and Simon also assumed that intelligence varied by gender and race as well. Again arguing for the importance of their work, Binet and Simon write:

> When the work, which is here only begun, shall have taken its definite character, it will doubtless permit the solution of many pending questions, since we are aiming at nothing less than the measure of the intelligence; one will thus know how to compare the different intellectual levels not only according to age, but according to sex, the social condition, and to race; application of our method will be found useful to normal anthropology, and also to criminal anthropology, which touches closely upon the study of the subnormal, and will receive the principal conclusion of our study. (1916, 92)

Thus the insistence that intelligence is being measured is necessitated by the presupposition that groups differ in intelligence, a theoretical proposition of profound importance, yet one not in any way necessary for the simple classification of students according to mental level, say based on some tasks performed at a clinic.[3]

With this, Binet and Simon moved from "measuring" a property of the individual to asserting a priori that this property was related to the group identity of that individual. They presumed that individuals—simultaneously naturally and social constituted—have intellectual properties that relate to their group, their social place, and their identity. IQ is thus a standard constructed on the basis of the link between the value of social positions and the value of individuals and groups. While Binet and Simon do not speak to the origin of racial or gender differences in intelligence (something clearly socially valued), to postulate them is to take a racist and sexist position, that is, a position asserting different social worth for individuals based on their group identity. These stands are obscured by repeated citations that Binet wished to help retarded children and improve their lot, a project not inconsistent, it should be noted, with Goddards' Training School at Vineland.

There is, then, a tendency to assert that there was a fundamental difference between Binet's thinking regarding intelligence and its measure, and how it was developed and applied within the United States. Critics and supporters of IQ testing similarly articulate this view. Underlying it is the argument that the original intentions, claims, and findings of Binet were sound and unproblematic.

An excellent example of this view is presented by Gould in his popular *Mismeasure of Man*: "All of [Binet's] caveats were later disregarded, and his intentions overturned by American hereditarians" (1981, 155; see also Schiff and Lewontin 1986, 8). It will be useful in this review, then, to carefully identify and examine Binet's intentions, ones that I will show are not contrary to the general IQ program in the United States. Gould argues that Binet's scores are a practical device that do not buttress any theory of intelligence and do not allow for "what they measure" to be designated as intelligence. Yet I will argue that Binet and Simon put forward a definite theory of intelligence, founded on a clear and relatively precise definition of intelligence. In short, Binet and Simon were very clear about what it was that they were "measuring." It was the requirements of theory that compelled Binet and Simon to insist on measurement, even as they acknowledged that such a stance was untenable. The scale, Gould also argues, "is not a device for ranking normal children" (1981, 155; see also Sarason 1976; Tuddenham 1962). While it is true Binet and Simon focused their efforts on the distinction between normal and retarded children, and between the various levels of retardation, there is nothing inconsistent in applying the test to "normal" populations, something Binet and Simon did, in fact, do (Nash 1990, chap. 2).

Gould concludes that the "misuse of mental tests is not inherent in the idea of testing itself" as developed by Binet (1981, 155). The weakness is his failure to analyze the standard of intelligence itself (insisting that it helped in the identification of his son's learning disability) focusing only on exposing unjustified interpretations and technical fallacies surrounding hereditarian claims (which are important contributions).

With a careful reading of Binet and Simon's tests, and an analysis of their social context, these interpretations will be challenged and a more complete understanding of the importance of this new standard will be put forward.

IQ Theory and the Secular Governance of Education

Although a maverick, by the turn of the century Binet was a well-known psychologist in France, with connections to and acquaintances with France's leading politicians. These connections were established as Binet led the Free Society for the Psychological Study of the Child, an organization inspired by the child study movement in the United States. Using it as a forum to influence matters of social and educational policy, and to encourage scientists to take up the study of social problems, Binet gained access to and respect from some of France's leading politicians and thinkers (Avanzini 1969).

The formation of the society was spearheaded by Ferdinand Buisson, then the chair of Science of Education at the Sorbonne. In 1902, Emile Durkheim, a founder of sociology and promoter of secular education and morality, was appointed deputy to Ferdinand Buisson, whom he succeeded in 1906, and was given responsibility for teaching the science of education. Buisson was also responsible for the reorganization of the primary schools as national director of elementary education (1879–1896). The reorganization sought to eliminate church control, making elementary education free and compulsory by the turn of the century. As the state gained control over education, it necessarily had to work out new policies and programs for France's schools. It was Buisson who asked Binet to participate in the society, and based on the support of Buisson, Binet became the society's energetic president. Binet, with Buisson, made conscious efforts to maintain connections with the Ministry of Public Instruction, and gain its support, financially and otherwise (Avanzini 1969, 40–43; Durkheim 1977, xi; *Encyclopedia Britannica*, 1999–2000 ed., s.v. "Bourgeois, Leon"). Binet's leadership in these areas led to his involvement in the commission that became the political impetus for the new test of intelligence.

It is useful to follow Binet's own recollection of the events surrounding the development of the new measuring scale of intelligence. He recalls:

> It was not until 1904 that the powers that be awakened from their indifference. The Minister of Public Instruction . . . appointed a Commission to study the abnormal—physical, mental, and moral—from the scholastic point of view. This Commission, over which M. Leon Bourgeois presided most ably, met a great number of times in 1904 and 1905, and drew up a complete scheme for the care and education of defective children, which has been embodied in a Bill by the Minister of Public Instruction. (Binet and Simon 1922, 6)

After noting the reluctance of the state to formally deal with "defective children," Leon Bourgeois wrote the following in his introduction to Binet and Simon's *Les enfants anormaux*.

> Yet, the obligation appeared to the state more and more clear to carry out all its duties toward the tears of nature: blind, deaf-mute, degenerate, retarded, unstable. What a sadness to think, for example, that children, to whom an original or acquired disability rendered instruction more precious and more necessary, are precisely those who are seen excluded from the benefit of school laws! (1922, v–vi)

Leon Bourgeois was a prominent French politician and statesmen, having briefly served as premier from 1895 to 1896. Bourgeois's introduction was written in 1907, when he was senator for the district of Marne, a post he held for nearly twenty years. As leader of the Radical-Socialist Party, with which Binet affiliated himself, Bourgeois stood as an anticleric and developed an influential social theory called "solidarism," which "stressed the quasi-contractual nature of society and the essential obligations of all men to it," an outlook reflected in Binet and Simon's writings. Significant in this regard was his book *The Politics of Social Planning* (*Encyclopedia Britannica*, 1999–2000 ed., s.v. "Bourgeois, Leon"; Stock-Morton 1988, 114–122). The premier during the time of the work of Binet and Simon was Emile Combes, also a member of the Radical-Socialist Party. Most important for his term was the separation of church and state. In 1895, he had joined the Leon Bourgeois government as minister of education. "When he left that post (April 1896), he remained active in politics and supported Pierre Waldeck-Rouseau's efforts to redefine the relationship between church and state." Succeeding Waldeck-Rouseau as premier in 1902, Combes "agreed to laws exiling almost all religious orders from France and dismantling major aspects of the church's public functions, especially in education," taking effect in 1905 (*Encyclopedia Britannica*, 1999–2000 ed., s.v. "Combes, Emile"). Thus, a major context for the commission's work was the transfer of control over education to the state, secularizing both its form and content.

Failure and the Secular Transformation of French Schooling

The commission and Binet, in particular, argued that "retardation" was a serious problem in France's schools. Binet expressed concern over the public's lack of attention to what he thought to be a crisis (Wolf 1973, 161). In a more public expression of their work, Binet and Simon outline the extent of this problem. "It is important to notice that the children so defined are not a negligible quantity," they warn. "And since number is the factor that gives importance to every social problem, we may say that the regulation of the lot of these children is a social question of the greatest gravity." After going through the various estimates of retardation in the schools—an effort frustrated by the lack of a common standard for its measure—Binet and Simon suggested that around 5 percent of the entire school population was retarded (1922, 7).

In particular, Binet and Simon expressed concern over the lack of a single standard for the measure of intelligence. Accuracy, they said, was essential not only for identifying the extent of the problem but also necessary for its remedy. In addition, a common measure of intelligence was required for the legitimacy of the institutions caring for both retarded and normal pupils while also serving to strengthen state authority over the schools.

Binet and Simon took for granted the already existing classification system or levels of "mental defectiveness"—the "idiot," the "imbecile," and the "moron." The problem was not with this obviously value-laden schema. "To be a member of a special class can never be a mark of distinction," Binet and Simon argue, "and such as do not *merit* it, must be spared the record" (1916, 10). According to this formulation, a child earns or deserves the various designations of normal, retarded, imbecile, and the like. Such language again admits to the assessment of social value.

For Binet and Simon, the main problem rested with variation in understanding and application of this terminology.

> Still among the numerous alienists,[4] under this common and apparently precise terminology, different ideas are concealed, variable and at the same time confused. The distinction between idiot, imbecile, and moron is not understood in the same way by all practitioners. We have abundant proof of this in the strikingly divergent medical diagnoses made only a few days apart by different alienists upon the same patient. (1922, 10)

"How will it be possible to keep a record of the intelligence in the pupils who are treated and instructed in a school," they continue, "if the terms applied to them, feeble minded, retarded, imbecile, idiot, vary in meaning according to the doctor who examined them?" (1922, 11). Again noting the problem resulting from the absence of a single standard, Binet and Simon write: "The simple fact, that specialists do not agree in the use of the technical terms of their science, *throws a suspicion upon their diagnoses*, and prevents all work of comparison" (ibid.; emphasis added). "But experience has shown how imprudent it would be to place *confidence* in . . . doctors who do not judge in exactly the same way, or who use different words to characterize the mental status of patients" (12; emphasis added). (Note that Binet and Simon identify such classifications as forms of judgment, not measurement.) Thus, the essence of the problem is that alienists disagree on the facts of classification, and for this reason they call for a precise basis for differential diagnosis in the form of psychological examinations (14; see also Wolf 1973, 141–154).[5]

Binet and Simon also warn of parents who feign the state of their child's intelligence, either to have them put into an institution or to avoid such an outcome. The new psychological tests were indispensable in overcoming this problem as well (1916, 39). The lack of a common standard, then, prevented analysis of the problem of retardation and undermined the legitimacy of the institutions responsible for children's care and instruction. On this basis, it makes sense to propose the development of a common standard as a solution. "Undoubtedly," then, "it would be a good work to bring about a unification of this nomenclature as has been done for the standard of measurements and for electric units" (1916, 14).

But classification was a priori, geared toward justifying differential socialization. The apparatus constructed by Binet and Simon rested, in part at least, on teachers' opinion of students. In discussing the procedure for determining the difficulty of the various test items and establishing age norms, the reader is told the following: "The masters were asked to designate only children of average intelligence, who were neither in advance of nor behind children of their own age, and who attended the grade correct for their years" (1916, 92). If the masters were able to designate children of average intelligence, why would one need to go to all the trouble of developing psychological instruments to "measure" intelligence? Likewise Thorndike suggested that the best neurologists could not correctly locate sixteen out of twenty as top or bottom students (Bracey 1995, 88). But I ask, if one knows who the top and bottom students are, who cares if the neurologists can tell? "Our use of the Scale was a surprise and a gratification," Henry Goddard wrote in the introduction to the volume he dedicated to Binet and Simon's work. "A classification of our children based on the Scale agreed with the Institution experience [sic]" (Binet and Simon 1916, 5). If it "agreed with the Institution experience" how was it of value and what information did it add?

As is consistent with the history of educational testing in general, this new test for the "measure" of intelligence finds its origin in the need to legitimate institutional practices and make credible those who work in them, as shifts in power arrangements take place, in this case the secularization of French schools. Political theory properly deals with the justification of relations of power, and the justification, the theory of power, embodied in Binet and Simon's instrument is in essence no different from that of Galton. The need was not for more or better information per se, but a standard process on which decisions about who gets what, when, where, and how could be based. Again revealing their concern with the problem of legitimacy when judging merit, Binet and Simon write, "Some errors are excusable in the beginning, but if they become too frequent, they may ruin the reputation of these new institutions" (1916, 10). If the intention is judging merit, legitimacy is key—for the type of schooling an individual receives is now bound up with the measure of their social worth, and in a merit-based society, it is those worth the most who get the most. This whole project is properly categorized as political and not psychological in nature.

It is instructive to review how Binet and Simon saw their work fitting into the larger social context and what they stated as their overriding motivations and preoccupations:

Amongst questions of present day interest, none are more discussed or attract a greater amount of attention than those which relate to social problems. The generous philanthropy of preceding generations seems to us to-day a little out of date, and we substitute for this virtue of the rich the otherwise fruitful idea that, by the very constitution of society itself, we are all in duty bound to occupy ourselves with the condition of our fellow-citizens, and especially of the less fortunate among them. This duty does not rest solely upon a sentiment of humanity. It is dictated equally by our own pressing personal interests; for unless, within a reasonable time, satisfaction is given to the just demands of the nine-tenths of society who are actually working for wages very little in harmony with their efforts and their needs, we already foresee that a violent revolution, from which the "haves" have very little to gain, will shake society to its very foundations. (1922, 3)

Bourgeois's social theory, influenced by the sociologist Emile Durkheim (Stock-Morton 1988, chap. 10), is evidenced in the emphasis on the "conditions of our fellow citizens" and its contractual nature (i.e., self-interest). It was this "nine-tenths" of the society that constituted the object of the new psychological examinations. From the previous quotation, it might also be inferred that the pronoun "our" does not refer to this group, but those experts and philanthropists who are being organized to address the threat of social revolution. Binet and Simon continue:

The consequence is that the very people who up to the present time have kept themselves most aloof from the social problems are being brought into contact with reality. It is a curious thing to see how scientific men, who for the past fifty years have never stirred a foot outside their laboratories, are showing a tendency to mingle in affairs. In spite of the diversity of the forces at work, there is one general fact which is undeniable. Pure and disinterested science retains its votaries, but the number is increasing of those who are turning to science for useful and practical applications; albeit, they are thinking less of science than of society, for it is those social phenomena which are capable of amelioration which scientific men are now studying by the most exact methods for the benefit of men of action, who are usually empirics. (1922, 2)

Binet and Simon reflect the new view of science emerging at the turn of the century, where experts are instrumental to social amelioration. The society established by Buisson and led by Binet was one concrete mechanism to involve scientists and professionals in policy, to "mingle in affairs." Binet goes on to note that such a program was already underway, evident among natural and social scientists.

Innumerable examples of this intervention of science in daily life might be cited. On the one hand, we see physiologists—Imbert, for example—who are setting themselves to the study of the phenomena of labor and the nutrition of different classes of workers, in order to find out whether the increase in wages and the diminution in the hours of work which the workers are forever crying for, can be justified by physiology. The day is not far off when such scientific observations, which are becoming more exact and more extensive, will play a part in the discussions between capital and labor.

Another example may be given of a different nature, but of identical significance. Psychologists are studying the value of evidence, and are thinking out better methods of arriving at truths, in order to discover reforms which may be introduced into the organization of justice. (1922, 2)

The role of the expert given here is clearly political—playing a part, for example, in the discussions between capital and labor. Psychologists in particular were studying the "value" of evidence (that is, its utility in class struggle); truth claims were examined in terms of their relevance for "reforms" aimed at the "organization of justice." What is significant is that the demand for higher wages and a decrease in the working day could not be justified unless experts deemed them appropriate. Workers had no legitimate claim without the advocacy of experts. Workers do not, as measured by the new tests, possess "good judgment." Thus, experts, those who could make "wise" decisions, played a mediating role between capital and labor.

The identification of the failure of groups of individuals to progress in school as a social problem developed in a context of a profound concern with the ability of existing institutions to address social problem more generally. Intelligence and its measure became an important tool in organizing schools to ameliorate social problems.

The Definition and Theory of Intelligence

In setting the grounds for the measure of intelligence, Binet made an explicit break with medical methods, arguing for the supremacy of the psychological method. He and Simon argued that intelligence is distinct from physical attributes and anomalies. "The child is judged to be an idiot because he is affected in his intellectual development," they explain. "This is so strikingly true that if we suppose the case presented to us where speech, locomotion, prehension were all nil, but which gave evidence of an intact intelligence, no one would consider that patient an idiot," later offering the example of Helen Keller (1916, 22, 43). With this they wanted to ignore physical deformities or irregularities, the appearance of which caused many intellectually normal children to be considered intellectually defective by physicians, and establish the classification of normal and subnormal children on the basis of intelligence alone. As well, Binet and Simon intended to distinguish between intellectual decay—as due to, for example, epilepsy—and inferior intelligence as such. After describing the two methods of identifying and looking at mental retardation, Binet and Simon suggested that the psychological method is the best because it "obliged the subject to make an effort which shows his capability in the way of comprehension, judgment, reasoning, and invention" (40).

Binet was not a proponent of operationalism, and for the most part he and Simon consistently employed a definition of intelligence as "good judgment" or "rectitude" (qualities given as faculties). Intelligence per se (what they came to call "rectitude of intelligence") is distinguished from intellectual level (what they came to call "maturity of intelligence") (1916, 259–261). Judgment in this case refers to having "good sense" and "sound judgment"; it refers to rational motives for beliefs or actions. "Rectitude" refers to "righteousness" as well as "correctness of judgment or procedure" especially "in the field of intellectual or artistic activity," according to Webster's. After rejecting perception and sensation as measures of intelligence, Binet and Simon offered the following conception:

> It seems to us that in intelligence there is a fundamental faculty, the alteration or the lack of which, is of the utmost importance for practical life. This faculty is judgment, otherwise called sense, practical sense, initiative, the faculty of adapting one's self to circumstances. To judge well, to comprehend well, to reason well, these are the essential activities of intelligence. (1916, 42)

"As a result of all this investigation," they continue on the next page, "in this scale which we present we accorded the first place to judgment." But it is not simply the ability to judge, to comprehend, to reason, that is the object—it is to do these things "well" that signifies the existence of intelligence. Assessing if something is done well is itself necessarily a judgment, while marking something as correct or incorrect is simply a point of fact. In the scale produced by Binet and Simon, both were evident.

When it came to naming colors or determining which weight is heavier, the focus was not only on the correctness of the replies, but the nature of the replies, the form they took. For example, it "is not certain errors which the subject commits, but absurd errors, which prove that he lacks judgment" (Binet and Simon 1916, 43). It is not the correctness of answers that primarily interest Binet and Simon, it is rather how a child answers the question that reveals the state of their intelligence. Their study of memory is a good case in point. In one such test, children were asked to repeat sentences that were carefully read aloud to them. "Not to repeat the whole is a lack of memory; to make absurd changes is an error of judgment" (108). In fact, Binet and Simon stipulated that encouraging absurdities is part of their method (43).

Another example is when Binet and Simon asked children to answer general questions, considered to test "comprehension." For example, "When one is in danger of being late, what must one do?" Replies were ranked explicitly as "good" or "bad," with examples given for each. Binet and Simon consider it absurd for children to reply, "We must start from home earlier." Or "We must bring an excuse from our parents." They write, after recognizing that many children did not interpret the question as they intended, "Our question means this: If one is already later than he ought to be, how can the lateness be diminished?" (1916, 225) Of course, charges of absurdity apply to Binet and Simon as well, for it makes little sense, one could argue, to suggest that there is a certain amount of lateness that "ought to be" and another that "ought not to be"—either one is late or they are on time. Nor does it make a great deal of sense, one could argue, to suggest that "lateness can be diminished" since if one is already late, that is a fact of history, and cannot be changed. The point is that Binet and Simon were looking for an answer they preferred—"I must hurry up, I must run"—but not one that is easily understood as being correct. Seriously answering the question probably depends on what one is late for, how often they've been late before, and for what reason they are late in the first place. This point is related to the general abstract or decontextual nature of the test.

Another good example of their notion of intelligence is given with their test "presentation of a picture" which they argued "renders invaluable service" and emphasized that if they had to retain only one test "we should not hesitate to select this one." This test is also used to "make a child talk." The main object of this test is to present a picture to a child, where they must "pass from the object to the word." "Here," they continue,

> the object is a picture, a scene full of meaning, containing a multitude of objects which he knows and at which he likes to look. Let us ask him to tell us what he sees. Not only will he talk and bring all of his vocabulary to bear upon the expression of his ideas, but he is free to look at and to choose what he pleases in the picture; he will therefore, show us what to him is most striking, and, at the same time, what idea directs him, what is his mentality, how he perceives, how he interprets, how he reasons. (1916, 188–189)

The pictures presented had a person and a theme. The child was instructed to tell the experimenter what he or she saw. Binet and Simon classified three types of replies—by enumeration (listing of objects), by description (actions with objects, e.g., "A man and a woman are sleeping on a bench."), and by interpretation (comments that go beyond what is visible). At this point, Binet and Simon justified the hierarchy they have constructed, where interpretation is designated as the highest mental level of the three. Their comments are very useful in understanding their dual notion of intelligence. They wrote:

> Since only older children attempt interpretation we are obliged to conclude that interpretation belongs to an intellectual level superior to that of description. But the question is complicated, for not only must attention be paid to the intellectual level but also to the deviations and errors which may occur in this same level. We recall having shown our pictures to an adult of whose stupidity we were well aware. His interpretations were many and of a peculiar order. For example, the first picture [a man and a boy pulling a cart] inspired the following reply: "It is a scene which is taking place in the month of February." Let us analyze this conjecture. It is evidently an interpretation, but without apparent foundation, and one that is impossible to confirm or to refute. The scene could have taken place equally well in October, November, December, January or even March [they are wearing coats]. Why then this precision which is so useless and unwarranted? The reply of this individual must be ranked among interpretations, and in our classification it is superior to the descriptive reply of a seven year old child; but, besides this, it displays a lack of judgment, and this lack of judgment is independent of this hierarchy of the replies. (1916, 194; see also 223–224)

First, with this Binet and Simon suggested a distinction between mental level and intelligence proper, and gave emphasis to their notion of intelligence as judgment. As well, it indicates the arbitrariness in determining what is good judgment; a decision ultimately resting with those who are making the judgments, a point that Binet and Simon do not miss. They parenthetically wrote that "it requires judgment to appreciate tests of judgment, and we hope not to have been entirely lacking" (1916, 129; see also 213–214).

Identification of the absurd is relative to place and time, context and culture, as is any judgment.[6] While this point does not need to be argued out with Binet and Simon's test of esthetic comparison—where children are asked to point to which portrait is "prettier"—this approach is also evident with their tests of arithmetic and color, tests that appear more objective (1916, 202–203, 276).

In one of the tests developed for five-year-olds, Binet and Simon asked children to count money. After placing coins in front of the child, the examiner is to say: "You see these *sous* [coins], count them; tell me how many there are." They explain as follows:

> Some children, without counting, answer immediately any number whatever; whether this answer is right or wrong, it is not taken into consideration, as the right answer might be given by chance. We insist that the child actually count with his finger. The slightest error suffices for considering that the test is not passed. (1916, 200)

What needs emphasis here is that for the child to get credit for this task, he or she must perform it as the experimenter demands, in addition to presenting the correct answer. In a similar test for nine-year-olds, children are asked to make change. In analyzing the various responses children make, Binet and Simon assigned high value to those who "take at once a ten-sou piece, to which they add six sous. Sometimes, like true merchants, they say, 'Four and tent sous are fourteen, and six more are twenty'. Sometimes they count in centimes. They are the virtuosos." Again, emphasis is given to the mode of expressing the answer, and the quickness in which it is provided, as well as whether the correct change is furnished (1916, 219).

Another example is found in the test "naming four colors" developed for eight-year-old children.

> Our test does not bear on the perception and distinction of the colors, but on their names, which is quite different. The young child distinguishes, recognizes, and easily matches without the least hesitation the most delicate shades of color, and has nothing to envy in the adult so far as his color sense is concerned; it is the verbalization of his color sense, if we may so express it, in which he is defective. (1916, 215)

Children are asked to name the four colors that appear on cards placed before them. They are asked, "What is the color?" Binet and Simon then insist: "No error is tolerated. The slightest error causes the test to be a failure" (1916, 215). No discussion is offered of what constitutes the "slightest error" but the the previous quote suggests that error is found in the "verbalization of his color sense." It seems possible that children who clearly articulate the correct color will receive more credit than those who mumble or hesitate in their answers, something Binet and Simon frowned on (see 107).

The point here is that the emphasis on judgment of answers as "good" and "bad" pervaded much of their scale, not just the more obviously culturally biased questions. More precisely, the main objective of the test constructed by Binet and Simon was to rank the value of the various responses according to different age populations.

Intelligence and Social Class

Binet and Simon noted that the tests that reveal the greatest difference between the social classes are those in which language plays a major part—it is these tests that are also said to tap the "spontaneous" or "natural" intelligence, an effect of the "rectitude" and not the "maturity" of intelligence. Even with these facts, Binet and Simon wrote:

> To sum up, the experiments of Decroly and Degand [who argued the scale was too easy for their well-to-do students] when thoroughly examined cannot lead us to change the tests; because if most of the tests have seemed too easy for their children, it is due simply to the fact that the intellectual level of their children is of the rich. (1916, 321)

Significantly, Binet and Simon asserted that groups—the rich and thus also the poor—have intellectual levels. The importance of this proposition cannot be overstated. It is an assertion that the intelligence of a person is related to their group identity, a frank admission that intelligence is bound up with the marking of social value. A few pages earlier, Binet and Simon again admitted their agnosticism toward the nature-nurture debate: "Is it a matter of heredity? Is it a matter of education? It would be difficult to establish a difference between the two factors which are here operating in conjunction" (1916, 318). Yet, either way, the rich have an intelligence superior, more valuable, to that of the working class. The test items most valued by Binet and Simon are the ones that reveal the most difference between the social classes. The items also are said to be the best measures for the "rectitude of intelligence."

But their definition of intelligence as "good judgment" or "rectitude" causes problems for their theory of intelligence, because it confuses consciousness with intelligence. Intelligence is defined as the ability to follow rules and recognize patterns, or more simply, the ability to learn. Yet, Binet and Simon took issue with this common conception.

> If one repeated it [any single test] two or three times it would disclose the following fact which we have often observed in

psychology; each pupil would present a slight gain as a result of practice from the re-examination, with an equal improvement for all, but proportionately larger for those whose results were poorest in the first trial; it would result from this that the seriation at each repetition would condense itself; there would be less individual difference, and the change would be especially marked among the weakest terms. It is therefore the lowest which gained most by the repetition; this seems paradoxical, *because one thinks of the ability to adopt oneself as a sign of intelligence*; and here it would rather be a *sign of mediocrity*. But it is easy to understand the reason; the intelligent adapt themselves quickly from the start, and they are thus almost immediately at their limit of adaptability; on the contrary the mediocre children adopt themselves less quickly, and consequently their progress is more visible. (1916, 109)

Thus, with this, they are admitting not to be concerned with the ability to learn, but with the value of already existing modes of thought.

That intelligence is often given as the ability to understand and comprehend suggests how ingrained the confusion is between the consciousness of individuals, resulting from the society they inhabit and their place in that society, and intelligence, a natural property not dependent on social relations. That is, human beings in general have a great capacity to learn, which is distinct from what it is that they learn, dependent on the society human beings live in. What any human being churns out during one of these tests is dependent on their society and their place in it. Thus, there is a problem in confounding properties of individuals—how fast they learn something—with what they learn, which is very dependent on their place, status, culture, and so on. Binet and Simon conflated these two by insisting that intelligence was a property of groups, and not simply a property that varied only among populations of individual human beings. The happy outcome of all of this is that those with good judgment are best suited for positions of power, and the standard for such judgment is those who already hold such power.

Summary

This chapter argued that with the rise in supremacy of the nation-state over ecclesiastical power, and its bureaucratic forms of administration and governance, the valuation of individuals rested increasingly on their talents and ability, attributes theorized to signify what was previously more openly sought—virtue and good character. Central to this shift was the development of the examination, especially examinations that sought to measure talent or ability, those functional mechanisms given as responsible for successful behavior or achievement.

The work of Binet and his colleague Simon needed to be reexamined as a result of evidence challenging common interpretations of Binet's work relative to the use of IQ tests in the United States. In particular, Binet and Simon were operating with the idea of organizing class society along lines of mental ability, and that such abilities varied along group lines, not simply among populations of individuals. I argued that the nature-nurture debate obscured this central feature of IQ theory, and suggested that for the theory it does not matter whether IQ scores are caused by genes or environment. The key lay in Binet and Simon's theorizing intelligence as a property of groups. Finally, the definition of intelligence offered by Binet and Simon was shown to actually be an assessment of judgment, breaking away from the more common understanding of intelligence as the ability to learn. This suggests that what is being assessed—that is, valued—is, in fact, the mode of thought: philosophy. The test is not primarily directed toward learning, or even "learning potential." Binet and Simon developed a standard whereby the value of people's thinking could be judged in a standard way, in a way that corresponded with the exigencies of social reproduction at that time. The final conclusion is then that those who have the best judgment are also those who hold positions of power, and therefore it is they who are the legitimate decision makers by virtue of their "good judgment."

8

Political Origins of Testing

This chapter identifies and discusses common features of the two case studies presented in the previous chapters. Common features suggest points of origin, and as such are helpful in exploring the impetus and significance of test-based initiatives such as No Child Left Behind.

Chapter 2 presented a heuristic for analyzing standards from the point of view of their role in establishing, maintaining, and extending political authority. As such, standards are instruments of political struggle. While serving both to legitimate and centralize power, established standards also reflect the values and interests of the dominant social class. As such, conflicts over standards point to struggles over what values and interests will reign supreme. And chapter 5 established that academic examinations were introduced to solve two definite, interrelated problems: (1) how to establish a legitimate social hierarchy in a society premised on an open class structure; and (2) how to institutionalize the role of reason in governance of public affairs and intellectual ability as a basis for political rights and participation. In both cases, these new standards were developed to address problems of authority, legitimacy, and outlook associated with the nation-building project of developing public school systems in France and the United States.

Mann and the Achievement Test

Representing the state and its newly kindled interest in education under the banner of the common school, Massachusetts' first secretary of education, Horace Mann, challenged the existing educational structure. The Boston schoolmasters were critical of Mann's progressive ideas, and struggled against his educational vision. Mann's ability to advance his agenda was facilitated by the board's adoption of competitive written exams. In the face of resistance, Mann intoned, "Scholars in the same school can be equitably compared with each other; and all the different schools are subjected to measurement by the same standard" (Kandel 1936, 26). Results of this endeavor provided Mann with information that "proved" the schools were ineffective. He was able to publicly discredit the schoolmasters who opposed his reforms.

Embodying new aims and functions, such exams necessarily clashed with the prevailing arrangements the Boston schoolmasters defended. Revealing their political nature, these exams helped shift accountability to the state and facilitate education reform. The shift in accountability was not, however, initially legislated. It was facilitated by establishing standards as the basis for collecting and presenting public information. And while Mann focused attention on the schools of Boston, he was, in fact, secretary of the Massachusetts Board of Education, and as such sought dominion over the schools of Massachusetts. His new exams constituted a weapon in the broader struggle to gain control over the entire "educational territory" by the state, chronicled by some as a quest for the "One Best System" (Tyack 1974).

Finally, the exams embodied American political theory articulated during the nation-building projects of the early nineteenth century. As far as the exam was concerned "all are born free and equal," an assertion that revealed the degree to which political theory guided educational practice. With this change, schools became an important location for associating political rights and economic opportunity with academic success.

With Mann, the new tests also functioned to mitigate disputes between schoolmasters and families who charge them with favoritism and the inevitable negative impact such charges have on the credibility of schools. In this way, the new exams were both a symbolic and practical means to bring "fairness" to public education.

Binet and the Intelligence Test

The French government commissioned Binet and Simon on the assumption that there was widespread retardation in the schools, and that special schools were needed for the "tears of nature." Practically, this intensified the need to classify students as normal or retarded. According to Binet and others, those who traditionally undertook this work—physicians and psychiatrists—were failing to establish such practice on a legitimate basis in that no common or objective standard for this work had yet been devised.

Binet and Simon presented their standard as a remedy for the tremendous variation in the diagnosis of intellectual "defectives." Like Mann, they were concerned that each physician used his own standard, and did so inconsistently, or subjectively. They were not simply developing a standard to be used in all the schools, however—other institutions such as courts and the military would find the new standard useful. But unlike Mann, they did calibrate their standard to a population on the basis of age. This was the main basis for their claim to have scientifically established a test that "measures" a child's intelligence; wittingly or unwittingly their procedure necessitated a close to normal distribution of scores that to many vindicated the view that some law was revealed by the use of the instrument.

One struggle that may also underlie the development of the new standard of intelligence was that between the medical and education practitioners and the emerging field of psychology. Binet and Simon emphasized the problems inherent in the medical and pedagogical methods for determining the intelligence of children, and not surprisingly criticisms leveled against their work came from medical doctors and teachers. In this way, the new standard of intelligence can be linked to what Wilson (1996) decries as a move from practitioner to expert knowledge as the basis for school evaluation, in that Binet's work assisted in shifting authority from educational or medical practitioners to expert psychologists and especially in the United States, psychometricians.

This initiative of the French state takes place in the context of the secularization of the French educational system and its premise of secular morality and public, not church, authority. And here, too, Binet and Simon's new standard has political content. Not only did the new standard of intelligence alter how equality of opportunity was conceptualized, it also corresponded to the rise of the expert in political affairs. No longer were all children to be given the same education—as Mann had advocated—rather specific curricula were attuned to their differing degrees of "intelligence," which could now be effectively "measured" and serve as an explanation of achievement differences. Central to this practice of tracking in education is the expert. The justification for expert status and power rests on the argument that some individuals have better judgment than others and thus they should receive training consistent with their future role as managers of the affairs of society. In particular, experts are needed for the management of human resources, including the determination of who could be an expert and who could not. This project is revealed in Binet and Simon's "ideal city," where "everyone would work according to his known aptitudes"—as assessed by expert psychologists. Schools increasingly became instrumental in this type of social engineering. Revealing their political function, experts are also given by French reformers as arbiters, between capital and labor for example. The illustration from chapter 7 is useful—experts were called on "to find out whether the increase in wages and the diminution in the hours of work which the workers are forever crying for, can be justified by physiology." Workers' demands alone would not suffice; they needed expert validation.

Common Features

With Mann, the problem was posed as not knowing with certainty the state of the schools, since different committeemen applied different standards when making school visitations. With Binet and Simon, a similar problem emerged when different alienists used different methods for the classification of mental state, all while using the same terms. Without the ability to compare individuals or institutions to a uniform standard, assessments about individuals or institutions were deemed illegitimate.

Thus, both Mann and Binet identified the lack of a common standard as the central problem and starting point for their reform efforts. Discourse about the need for common standards in these contexts is derived from quests for accountability, defined by Wiggins (1993) as comparability on common measures. In both cases, lack of a common standard signaled a legitimacy crisis for the relevant institutions and the professions that operated them—it was not clear what standard or rule was at work, and when it was, the standard was deemed improper. What is important here is that standardization is given as part of a political theory (how to justify decisions about who gets what, when, where, and how), having a different meaning from that used in the sphere of production or scientific experimentation. While it makes sense, for example, to insist that people meet the same specific requirements before they are awarded a professional license, standardization emerges in the context of compulsory public education as a means to legitimate both "opportunity" decisions and accountability to a state power. This type of standardization is the more general type—"to cause to conform to a standard."

In this way, both efforts claim political neutrality via the uniform application of a standard as a guard against factional or partisan influence in either opportunity decisions or the use of public power. Having identified the lack of a common standard as a problem, Mann and Binet saw a solution in the application of the same standard to all under their purview, and in this regard, standardization can be seen as a key component of the new standard and its claim to equality. Both Mann and Binet justified their new standard and the shifts in power it entailed with the claim that it would prove a more reputable basis for making judgments about schools and individuals. With Mann, exams were more fair, more just, and a more accurate way to judge the performance of schools. With Binet, intelligence tests contributed to the efficient organization of society, where "no particle of psychic force should be lost for society." Likewise, in both cases, the exams were part of a larger initiative to deal with concerns about growing inequality and social unrest.

Also common to both cases, and most significant for this study, is the use of new academic tests to present information that supports reformers' charges that existing institutional arrangements were failing. These claims served to push reforms initiated before the development of the new tests with the test-derived information serving not as the basis of decisions, but rather as a justification for them (the need for changes in school governance and curricula; the need for special education and educational tracking). In both cases, this failure was both in terms of performance (schools failing to teach reason; schools failing to assist intellectually abnormal students) and in terms of legitimacy (teachers favoring students of prominent citizens; classifying an individual as intellectually defective).

As well, in both cases the use of standards in the form of academic tests limits the power of one group in favor of another. In this way, it can be said that standards are used to sort out conflicting claims or interests. In the case of Mann, local schoolmasters—the then-existing "educational establishment"—lost power, and the state used the information produced by the new exam not only to bring educators under closer supervision of the state, but also to justify that new power by presenting it as an equitable basis for resolving conflicts. Further, both cases reveal the use of standards for presenting the state as a neutral means to sort out conflict, where, for example, the interference of teachers in student assessments or the self-serving acts of parents regarding the mental state of their child would be controlled. With the new standards, fairness became an important criteria, and as such, the new standards were given as more legitimate.

Interestingly both cases show a refusal to examine failure from alternate perspectives. Mann refused to consider students' intelligence as a factor in their performance, even though he was steeped in phrenology and its premise of constitutional variation in human character and intellect. Teachers and school organization and not individual traits were to blame, an approach very similar to the present mantra of "all students can learn." A priori, Binet and Simon insisted that failure to progress in school was the result of a weak intelligence. Other factors that might contribute to school "retardation" such as an irrelevant and limited curriculum, poor teaching, and the impact of poverty were not considered. Perhaps significant numbers of those attending French schools at the end of the nineteenth century were not native French speakers. Yet instruction was, nonetheless, in French (Weber 1976, 204–338).

In both cases, the new standards functioned as tools in the assessment of social value. Changes in standards for education initiate changes in the aim and philosophy of education. Put another way, efforts to change a standard reflect efforts to change power relations, as well as the aims and values guiding social practice. If this is true, the new standards developed by Mann and Binet should reflect new aims and values.

With Mann, the emphasis of the new standard was not only on assessing the individual student, but also on the content and methods of instruction. By assessing the students' academic achievement, Mann determined the value of the content and form of their instruction, developing one mechanism to enforce a progressive ideology. With the justification Mann offers for the new tests, one can readily see Kula's propositions at work. Ideas surrounding standards often reflect social theories about justice and equality;

an excellent example of this is Mann's focus on being "equal" before the test.

Corroboration of Kula's observation that the fineness of a standard reflects the value of the object for that particular culture or society is found in the case of both of Mann and Binet. By increasing the fineness of the measure to allow for a greater range of achievement, Mann increased the value of the preferred school-based knowledge and, by extension, those who evaluated that knowledge. Put another way, increasing the differentiating power of the standard reveals that the object of the standard has increased in value. Binet's measure of intelligence was also premised on greater power to differentiate and in turn provided evidence of the utility of empirical science over religious dogma for guiding the affairs of society.

These new standards signaled what the state did and did not value. The fact that the students under the masters' tutelage did so poorly is a reflection of the fact that they were being held accountable to a different standard than they were operating under, one that reflected a different philosophy of education. With Binet's standard of intelligence came a host of assumptions about the proper way to organize society, including a new basis for morality and the structure of education.

In general terms, the struggle in France was similar to the struggle between religious sects and the state during the common school reforms in the United States (see Glenn 1988). In both cases, exams were yet one more means by which the state gained further control over the organization and content of schooling. It seems very significant that both Mann and Binet were actively abetting the state's struggle to gain control over education from religious or local communities and impose a particular outlook (e.g., the ideology of the Whig Party or the Radical-Socialist Party's "solidarism"). The evidence of values in the development of competitive written exams warrants more consideration. The conclusion that Binet and Simon were judging the value of different modes of thought or consciousness points to the problem of values in general, secular or religious. The emphasis exams now place on values may be a vestige of their origins in religious institutions and role in secularization. For example, Montgomery (1967) charts how the examination systems in England developed within the church-controlled universities of Oxford and Cambridge—yet these instruments, modified, become tools of the state in the end.

One weakness in the case study is that the actual items on Mann's test were not analyzed. The study would have benefited from such an analysis, as I think it did with the analysis of Binet and Simon's test items. It was noted, however, that Mann emphasized the importance of reason, lamenting its absence in some of the answers furnished by students. Despite this weakness, however, it is possible to see that valuation is clearly at work. Recall that Mann and Binet were insistent on comparison. The fact that the prevailing system did not allow for comparison of schools or individuals on a "fair" and "objective" basis was a major problem posed by both reformers. Mann's new standard allowed schools to be compared against a common standard. Binet's new standard enabled individual intelligence to be examined in light of an age norm. In both cases, these practices were deemed fair and objective on the basis that all were examined using the same standard. It must be understood that the actual aim and outcome of such comparison was the ranking of schools or individuals along a single continuum of "best" to "worst." Such a continuum is not, in fact, measurement. Ranking students from "good" to "bad" is evidence of a system for the making of social value. It is important to recall that social value deals with the linkage between structural position (high or low rank in this case) and moral worth or goodness (virtue).

Mann set up a system in which the value of the output of the schools could be determined on the basis of such comparison. Emulation or place-seeking were to be replaced with competitive standards set by the state. Note too that both Mann and Binet gave fairness and competition as values. The value of fairness was achieved by being "value neutral." Competition is also given as a value, in that those that excel in marketlike conditions (i.e., the social sphere is modeled on the economic sphere) are valued more than those that do not excel under such conditions. Such valuation is not scientific in nature, even if scientific technique is involved in its production. Pronouncements of superiority and inferiority, good and bad, are in the domain of values and presume a values system. They should be understood as distinct from factual or theoretical knowledge (which is not to say that such phenomena are unrelated). Finally, the values appear as class values, as emanating from definite interests. Little mistake could be made that fair and open competition for social prestige and power are values of the capitalist class as it emerged victorious in its fight against landed aristocracy and the authority of the church.

Summary

Thus, with both Mann and Binet, there was a struggle over the standard to be employed in the sphere of education and the standard, again in both cases, did embody political theory. Educational standards were, in both countries, implicated in establishing and maintaining a definite political order and embodied the value system of those who led reform.

9

The Failure of Testing

The Nature of the Problem Revisited

The academic examinations advanced by Mann and Binet were part of a larger drive to solve problems associated with establishing a society that valued social difference (rank and class) yet rejected a fixed-class structure based on bloodlines. Fundamental to the establishment of this new social order—what we understand as democratic political institutions and free-market economies—is a contradiction: the declaration of formal equality among all adult members of the society and the reality of structured inequality and value of social difference. The premise of formal equality stands with great tension against the reality of real inequality, the historical solution to this being the notion of equity—fair competition to acquire scarce social, political, and economic privilege. Included in this arrangement is the formation of a public and public sphere for the edification and expression of public opinion and reasoned debate as well as a means for the selections of those best fit to govern and manage the affairs of society.

Public school systems emerged in part to institutionalize public means to address these tensions and bring stability to the new political structures. But the new exams were not only imbued with this outlook—they were imbued with the contradictions inherent in the political and economic system itself: all can succeed yet there exists historically unprecedented social inequality. Hence, we have the psychometric practice of equal treatment as a basis for social differentiation.

The failure of testing might simply be evident in the following claims. Far from being able to "close the achievement gap" and promote opportunity for minorities, "standards-based" reforms have so far resulted in the opposite of the rhetoric that supports the practice: more and more children are "left behind" as dropouts appear to be increasing and curriculums have narrowed as (mostly) working-class and minority youth are condemned to a regime of test-prep and little more. Standards-based reform has failed to bring about fair, equal educational opportunities, failed to improve schooling, and even failed to provide accurate information on the state of public schools (e.g., Apple 2001; Bracey 2002; Fuller, Wright, Gesicki, and Kang 2007; Haney 2000; McNeil, Coppola, Radigan, and Heilig 2008; Nichols and Berliner 2007; Orfield and Kornhaber 2001; Pile 2005; Popham 1999; Saltman 2000 2005; Woestehoff and Neill 2007).

But this might only connote failure of policy. But more is at stake. Standardized tests of achievement and ability no longer serve as a solution to the historic problems noted previously, that is, liberal notions of opportunity and public governance have failed to block the emergence of gross inequality and the illiberal (monopoly) private dictate of public affairs.

The Nagging Problem of Inequality

While it is clear that standardized testing has its origin in the rise of liberal democracy against feudal aristocracy, it is also clear that this new order, and the standards it gave rise to, failed to break with certain key aspects of the feudal order. Thus, the question posed in chapter 2, namely, whether standardized tests are representational or conventional measures, helps us understand the contradictions inherent to standardized testing outlined in this chapter.

The representational status of our current assessment tools is revealed in their fixation on social value—the linking of individual place to social slot in a hierarchical and increasingly unequal social system. Like the rigid feudal society that predated them, testing techniques are fixated and validated on their link to unequal social structure while employing procedural equality through standardization. They were able to buy time for liberal political arrangements by transforming the process of marking social value to one that is "open" and "equitable" and undertaken and arbitrated by "neutral" authorities, while in fact structuring inequality on a historically unprecedented scale. Unlike fixed-class or caste systems, everyone had the right to the opportunity to be marked worthy or unworthy; the individual's mental attributes were given as a natural (unbiased by social hierarchies) means by which to assign social value.

This contradiction is evident in the project of "closing the achievement gap." The policy of closing "the achievement gap" is a legacy of the theory of natural distinction, although current policy works the theory backward. While academic achievement and ability were given as a natural basis for social distinction, today's project seeks to remedy the overgrowth of social inequality by closing gaps in academic performance, that is, minimizing "natural" differences as evident in academic achievement.

But this strategy fails because social difference does not have its origin in natural difference for the simple fact that human beings are one group, not a collection of naturally occurring subgroups, or "races." Variation among individuals is, in fact, a within-group phenomenon (see Schiff and Lewontin 1986). Social differences are social in origin, and have no basis in "natural" distinctions of intelligence or even strength as social value distorts history by abstracting individuals from their social reality.

The achievement gap's irrationality is a legacy of this theory. Attempting to equalize school outcomes via measures that presume to differentiate is nothing if not irrational. Closing gaps in intellectual performance—that is, in equalizing outcomes—will not solve the problem of what are now unsustainable social inequalities because these social inequalities do not have their origin in intellectual difference. Put another way, the current emphasis on "achievement gaps" in the context of fundamental social inequality stands on the assumption that it is group differences in intellectual performance that undergird inequalities of wealth and status, and in this way, a singular emphasis on closing "achievement gaps" in such a context will serve only to exacerbate educational and social inequality. Historical experience has thus proven the theory of "natural distinction" wrong and the impotence of "equity" remedies to address class antagonism. As long as they are laden with the presupposition noted earlier, policy efforts to improve the quality and level of education for all will fail.

Legitimacy and the Credibility of Authority

The use to which Horace Mann put his new standard of academic achievement is strikingly similar to the limited yet influential role of the National Commission on Excellence in Education (NCEE) and its report *A Nation at Risk* (1983). In many ways—though certainly not all—Mann's efforts foreshadowed the power afforded standardized tests in bringing about the radical restructuring of public education under the No Child Left Behind Act (NCLB).

While Mann crafted an educational theory premised on addressing social inequality and establishing public responsibility for providing equal opportunity, and social and political unity—that is, the new and expanded government role in education was the response to the failure of the old institutional arrangements—*A Nation at Risk* and the No Child Left Behind Act identify public education as the source of various economic and political problems. Mann's efforts were representative of a trend to empower government as an agent of public power and defender of the public good. While NCLB also represents a trend to expand federal power, it is an agent of private monopolies who will yield public benefits with the utmost efficiency and accountability to the "customer."

Possibly no other single policy event in the last fifty years corroborates the observation that test data are used to confirm failure more than the publication of *A Nation at Risk*. Since its publication (and even before, see Bracey 1995), the consistent message of top- ranking government officials, CEOs, and supposedly politically neutral think tanks, foundations, academicians, and media have been that the U.S. public education system is in decline. The "educational establishment" and its defense of "government schools" finds itself in a position similar to that of the Boston schoolmasters of 150 years ago: unwilling to submit to the new regime, it faces public exposure of failings through the publication of test-derived data, the main mechanism for discrediting professional educators and the institutions they serve. Tests become a pretext for a radical shift in how education is governed, and the purpose it serves. According to some well-known observers, production of this bad news has itself become an industry and means by which to build one's academic career (Bracey 2002).

A Nation at Risk (hereafter *Risk*), as many will recall, blamed education for various economic and political maladies. Albeit with intellectual bad faith, *Risk* presented some test results to prove its thesis that the level of education in the United States had dramatically declined putting the "nation at risk." Its modus operandi was fear, outlining with military language and metaphor the nature of the risk and how to fight the enemy of mediocrity with the "ideals of excellence." *Risk* was premised on accepting the vision of the United States as world empire ("America's destiny"), a main theme few critics spoke to, choosing instead to debate that which the commission had admittedly no fidelity: facts.

In then-Secretary of Education Terrance Bell's memoir, *The Thirteenth Man*, he is candid about that commission. It did not aim to objectively examine the condition of U.S. public education, but to document the bad things Bell had heard about the public schools (see Bracey 1999). Commission member William O. Baker's admission that "we disregarded what we didn't believe," when questioned about conflicting National Assessment of Educational Progress data (Hlebowitsh 1990, 85), best exemplifies the approach now taken to school "reform". Not caring what the facts are is not limited to one reigning family in U.S. politics or debates about the Middle East. When examining the rise of standardized testing, one is struck at just how common this approach to educational policy is (see Airasian 1988).

This again points to the problem of credibility that standardized tests were engineered to address. Importantly, credibility is the ability to inspire belief or trust. This problem of credibility appears in the case of both Mann and Binet, as their new tests were used to bring into question the credibility of existing practices, and the need for new arrangements. Tests in both instances signified and enabled a removal from power of one group—the Boston schoolmasters and individual clinicians, in the case of Binet—by calling into question the established practices of the group losing power. In fact, the British sociologist Patricia Broadfoot observes that political accountability is emphasized during times when the legitimacy and credibility of a government is at issue (1996; see also Trow 1996).

But Bell's statement not only reveals that the commission was not interested in a serious and objective investigation into the state of public education. It also reveals that the commission existed to establish a nonrational basis for policy formation. The efficacy (or value) of the existing system was to be officially challenged, but not by facts as facts, but by facts as assertions. It is a move that simultaneously disregards test data while relying on the social artifact of tests to establish boundaries for discussion and policy formation.

The original appeal of test data was that of its utility for public reasoning about school quality. Such acts are premised on the idea that the merits of an argument are to be based on judgments of reason or fact, not the social status or position of those making the argument or presenting the facts. Now things have turned around: test data mean what those in power say they mean; the merits of argument are to be determined by examining the social status of those making the argument.

Thus, the basis of the belief that formed the assertions originated with the authority of NCEE and the federal government. Bell's assertion, and assertions such as "I don't care what the facts are" by those who occupy the Office of the President are aimed at establishing credibility on a nonrational basis. They give credibility, from the Latin "worthy to be believed," as originating in authority as opposed to being derived from reason, as Thomas Hobbes (1909) and those who followed him argued in their fight against irrationalism. The role of authority, for these officials, is the production of belief as social fact. Because the standards that Mann and Binet fought for were designed to support a predetermined agenda—as pretexts for reform—they would inevitably fail to block the irrationalism of *Risk*.

Based on a commentary from *New York Times* reporter Ron Suskind, one can see that this outlook regarding authority as the source of belief is at work at the highest echelons of governance. Suskind writes:

In the summer of 2002, after I had written an article in Esquire [*sic*] that the White House didn't like about Bush's former communications director, Karen Hughes, I had a meeting with a senior adviser to Bush. He expressed the White House's displeasure, and then he told me something that at the time I didn't fully comprehend—but which I now believe gets to the very heart of the Bush presidency.

The aide said that guys like me were "in what we call the reality-based community," which he defined as people who "believe that solutions emerge from your judicious study of discernible reality." I nodded and murmured something about enlightenment principles and empiricism. He cut me off. "That's not the way the world really works anymore," he continued. "We're an empire now, and when we act, we create our own reality. And while you're studying that reality—judiciously, as you will—we'll act again, creating other new realities, which you can study too, and that's how things will sort out. We're history's actors . . . and you, all of you, will be left to just study what we do." (2004, 51)

Several things are particularly noteworthy. Executive authority is given as the only legitimate doer (remember this is coming from a spokesperson for the White House). Its credibility is derived not from reason or law, but from the act of doing itself, the creation of "new realities." For those under the yoke of this empire, including those attending schools in the United States, study of the actions of the authority is their only role, where study (from the Latin *studium*), for zeal or affection, denotes awe on the part of subjects. Subjects' own actions, powers, and desires are not recognized except as extensions of actions of the empire. This contention is important to keep in mind when thinking about the chapters on the political basis of psychometry. But it is also important to keep in mind more generally, as the outlook revealed by *Risk* and Suskind denies any legitimate role for the public, for active public participation in governance.

Independent action of subjects cannot be recognized in this framework, overthrowing the "individual" that was placed at the center of the social order during the rise of the bourgeoisie and its Enlightenment against absolutist monarchy. What Suskind outlines presents credibility as originating in the use of force or power: authority is that which "authors life" (to "author" is "to make to grow, originate") and of course this includes the power to take life away. The life of schools and those who inhabit them increasingly turns on test scores, or is "authored" by them.

While NCLB also operates through the logic of fear and a disregard for what the facts are, the current standards movement operates under a much broader discourse of failure than *Risk* ever did. There is now a not-so-subtle subtext pervading official discourse that says public education, as both a system and an ideal, is a failure. The authors of *Risk*, unlike the promoters of NCLB, did not present "reform" via privatization (though apparently a section of those in Reagan's Department of Education wanted vouchers to be offered as a solution; see Bracey 2002). Implied in the commission's report was hope for at least a conservative brand of public education and the traditional goals it served, both in terms of citizenship, opportunity, and economic productivity. While *Risk* spoke to fairly broad notions of opportunity, NCLB has as its mobilizing theme "closing the achievement gap" (which by logic, it should be noted, could be achieved by lowering the level of top-performing schools), claiming its mandate originates, not on the defense of the nation, but with the civil rights of those who have historically been "poorly served" by public schools in the United States.[1] Note here that there is a shift from the external—the risks are external in nature, for example, global competition—to the internal: the failure of the quintessential American promise of opportunity for all.

One of the most interesting things about today's education deformers[2] is their co-optation of left-leaning critics of public education, who for almost a century emphasized the role of public schools in reproducing various forms of social, political, and economic inequality (for an example of this see Hess 2002). While these earlier critics' evaluations of public education are aimed at insisting it live up to the democratic ideals on which it ostensibly stood, the trend over the past two decades has been to argue that the shortcomings of public education result from inherent flaws in the system and the idea of public education itself (e.g., the notion of "government schools" pushed by neoconservatives is aimed at discrediting public education). Along with this is the common perception among educators that the results of the demands of NCLB will be nothing short of the elimination of public education "as we know it," since the law mandates charter schools, for-profit school management, and state takeovers for not complying with what are widely recognized as the law's impossible and arbitrary demands (Bracey 2002).[3] Recent analyses claim that by 2014, the vast majority of public schools in the United States will be deemed failures by NCLB (National Education Association, 2005, 2006). This failure will shift control of education to for-profit educational management organizations, tutoring agencies, and test-prep companies and other commercial endeavors.

The power that stands behind the so-called standards movement, exemplified by the NCEE as outlined earlier, is in essence arbitrary; the standard it wields is arbitrary, or at least wielded in an arbitrary way. Possibly the most important example of this is the National Assessment of Educational Progress (NAEP). The NAEP plays an important role in further limiting states' authority and credibility, for, under NLCB, NAEP scores are the final arbiters of progress. NAEP data will be used to contend that states are lying to their citizens about school progress and serve to further justify the "education industry." Yet NAEP "achievement levels" are themselves arbitrary (Bracy 2003, 2–4; see also Epstein 1998).

While NCLB supporters routinely point out that the law itself does not use the word *failure*, preferring instead to insist on a series of euphemisms, it is clear from their own documents that NCLB, in fact if not in name, is labeling many public schools failures.[4] Both the big commercial news agencies and government officials at all levels increasingly speak about public schools as failures and now openly trumpet privatization as the solution. As Bracey (2002) points out, this is far from a conspiracy since it is an open (public) goal, enshrined in public law and publicly articulated by both government officials and business elites. NCLB-induced failure will necessarily result in a vast expansion of the education industry in the United States., and hence a fundamental transformation of the form, content, and function of education in the United States. The move toward privatization is no longer speculation by radical critics.

Unlike past episodes in the expansion of standardized testing, however, the current emphasis on testing is rooted in the failure of liberal democracy itself, not its construction and expansion as in the past. While variously designated as neoliberalism, privatization, and the right wing's "war on terrorism," the failure of liberal democracy is evident in the dismantling of social responsibility (especially for education) and the turning over control of all that is public to private monopolies, which are subsidized and protected by governments, who are increasingly, it should be noted, also characterized by unbridled and militarized executive authority. Evidence and critical discussion of this shift is voluminous and multifaceted (e.g., Apple 2001; Bernstein 2001; Giroux 2004; Johnson 2007; Saltman 2000, 2005), but noteworthy is the role academic tests are now playing in the open attack on and radical restructuring of public education as a bulwark of American democracy.

Testing and the Radical Restructuring of Public Education

In the book *Who Governs Our Schools*, Conley argues that a "revolution is taking place." "That revolution," he continues, "is the reshaping of power and authority relationships at all levels of the educational governance and policy system. Although this revolution began perhaps 30 years ago, its pace and intensity accelerated during the 1990s" (2003. 1). The Education Commission of the States' report "The Changing Landscape of Educational Governance" (1999) buttresses this argument, although without explicitly doing so. And just as was the case with Mann and Binet, academic standards are playing an important role in bringing about and justifying the reshaping of these power relationships.

The content to this "revolution"—which is better characterized as wrecking in that it is patently designed to dismantle a bulwark of American democracy—is twofold. There is a concentration of power in the hands of executive bodies at all levels of government: city and municipal, county, state, and federal. This is evidenced by mayoral control of schools and regionalization schemes. Accompanying new state and federal testing regimes is a general extension in the reach of state and federal power; hence the objection of state's rights and local control interests to the now infamous No Child Left Behind Act. Concomitant to this concentration of power is the move to eliminate elected governance as a norm. Witness the emasculation of school boards in cities with mayoral control such as Chicago and New York, as well as where the state has taken over a school district, as was the case with New Jersey. For some time now both neoconservatives and new-democrats alike have been agitating to broaden this trend, acting to curtail if not eliminate school boards (e.g., Finn 2004; Ravitch and Viteritti 1997). The elimination of elected governance and concentration of power in the hands of executive bodies has generally preceded privatization schemes, as is the documented case with Chicago (Lipman 2002).

While state and federal agencies have claimed more power over education, especially with NCLB, responsibility for the actual provision of education—in particular its funding—has been reduced and/or redirected toward the "education industry." In short, while the government is claiming more and more power over education, it is simultaneously shirking responsibility for the provision of that education, trumpeting instead the market values of individual responsibility and choice. This represents nothing short of a massive shift in the roles and responsibilities of government in terms of education. It is my contention that this shift signals a momentous change in the role formal schooling is to play within the larger political system of the United States, and the very nature of that political system. However limited, public education served as a mechanism to place limits on government power, served as a means to block one faction from dominating all others, and served as a means to legitimate and extend the role of public opinion in governance. Far from extending this drive and placing it on a modern footing, the current standards movement is part of a larger trend to eliminate representative democracy and also signals the possibility of civil war as the clash between ruling factions intensifies. That public agencies for limiting the power of any one faction and for promoting "national unity" are being privatized only weakens mechanisms blocking civil war and for the formation of a national citizenry.

As a measure, then, standardized tests now reflect a power that also appears to be failing as neither military rule or civil war are particularly stable and reproducible political arrangements. As this tool is part of an effort to seek more federal control over more of the education landscape, continued resistance seems imminent on the legal, political, and social fronts (e.g., Krone 2008; Walsh, 2008). Far from constituting a basis for resolving conflicts as was the case with Mann and Binet, current test-based initiatives appear to be failing to generate clear victory for one faction, a viable alliance between factions, or to secure compliance of educators (e.g., Rothstein 2007).

Testing has also failed to convince the population of the utility in ignoring the social context of schooling, as market assumptions of individual responsibility and choice are largely unpopular when they take the form of public votes. The public may be prepared to reject the founding premise of "natural merit" as a basis for social organization. While "as far as the test is concerned" all may be "free and equal," the historical structured and growing inequalities in health care, housing, education, and so on, remain and are increasing. Testing has not contributed to their disappearance. This reality as a reality of the present political economy haunts the promoters and crafters of high-stakes testing reform who trumpeted their support for those historically ill-served by public schools.

Summing Up and Thinking about Alternatives

The long-standing debate as to whether standardized tests accurately measure merit (worth) is simultaneously a frank admission that standardized tests aim to assign value to human beings—to determine who is worthy of what type of education—and a block to grasping fully the significance and implications of such a project. Standardized tests are not designed to accurately and fairly select, certify, and monitor via measurement of specific competencies or abilities, but rather to legitimate such acts via the assessment of social value. Thus, it may be more useful in analyzing psychometry to view it as political theory, as a formal justification for a system where "the argument for democracy is not that it gives power to men without distinction, but that it gives greater freedom for ability and character to attain power" (E. L. Thorndike quoted in Karier 1973, 122).

Possibly the first implication of this understanding is to reject any form of assessment that functions to differentially value human persons. Let me be clear: the issue is not in recognizing that humans differ in their abilities, interests, and so on (though such differences are not, in my view, the problem they can be made out to be). The problem emerges when such differentiation is systematically linked to a hierarchical social structure and the reproduction of that structure.

Thus, there is a need for assessment in education to establish a new starting point, one predicated on the equal worth, dignity, and rights of human beings and human cultures. Those working to develop assessments in the service of education must vociferously reject the linking of academic prowess with notions of bad or good. The habit of talking of good students must be replaced with a culture in which the work of teachers, students, and the community as a whole is judged by teachers, students, and the community as a whole on the basis of whether this collective work is serving to prepare youth to solve the problems they and their society face. This is the basis on which assessments should take place, and in fact such a drive may underpin recent efforts toward alternative or authentic assessment, in particular those predicated on Gardner's (1993) notion of multiple intelligences, which opens up space to recognize and value a broad range of human abilities and achievements.

This conclusion has implications for the present standards and accountability movement, especially as embodied in NCLB. It suggests to me that strategies opposing NCLB on the basis that it does not provide enough funds to meet legal requirements misses the fact that NCLB, and in particular its testing mandates, are in themselves attacks on public education and those who attend and work in public schools. Based on what has been presented here, the law's functioning to mark so many of the nation's schools as failures is not an aberration. By marking public schools as failures, this standards-based reform in my view is devaluing public education and education itself. It is an effort, among other things, to assimilate Americans to a lower standard of education, not to a higher one. It is a clear message by those in power that the arrangement whereby all are to have the quintessential American opportunity of education is being wrecked, replaced with the notion that only those who "perform well" deserve an education.

Education, after all, is a right, a claim on society based on no other consideration whatsoever except that of being a human being, the claim being valid and legitimate as a modern quality education is a requirement for the performance of one's responsibilities to the society.[5] This study finds that standards cannot exist outside a definite political system, or put another way, a new authority must come into being and bring with it, as all authorities do, a set of standards that represents its interests and serves to establish its power. For standards and assessments that genuinely advance the interests of all youth and educators, an authority must come into being that, in kind, represents these general interests, and is of these general interests. Absent this kind of broad political change, real advances in educational practice and theory are drastically limited.

This does not mean, however, that educators, parents, students, and youth have no role but to "wait for change," or simply oppose "standards." Possibly the most significant conclusion educational practitioners, community leaders, and youth might take from this analysis is the necessity for them to take up as practical educational and political work the establishment and fight for standards. For in taking up the very concrete and difficult work of determining and fighting together for standards to assess schools and all those who work in them, the interests and outlook of all involved will be represented and, in the end, protected. No one should shy away from the political nature of standard-setting; instead, they should embrace the need to fight over standards as the political and philosophical conflict that it is. Broadly involving people in discussions about standards, will counter the exclusion of and dissolution of the public, and the general and particular interests of various groups it must serve. After all, it is not standardization as such that threatens education, but rather the centralized, unelected executive, and increasingly private, control over academic exams in the service of a very narrow vision for education that is the issue. In the end, vision must be contended with as concrete work, and what better way to map out another world and the means and ends of education than through an active fight over standards used in judging the work of schools.

Notes

Preface

1. A good resource for information on the resistance to standards-based education reform and a listing of organizations opposed to "high stakes testing" has been compiled and published by George Schmidt, former veteran Chicago Public School teacher, who was fired for his opposition to Chicago's testing regime. This can be found at http://www.substancenews.com/archive/links.htm.

2. There are two definitions of standardized test, one more restrictive than the other. The first notion refers simply to giving all students the same questions, under the same conditions, all to be scored by the same rubric. A more strict definition holds that to be standardized, a measuring instrument must be calibrated to a population or "norm referenced."

1. A Measure of Failure

1. I say "as we know it" in response to reformers' efforts to create confusion over what constitutes public education, a notable example being the claim that "charter schools are public schools." If this is so, why the name "charter"? Charter schools and other market-based reforms constitute a radical change in the conception and organization of schooling in the United States.

2. Unless otherwise noted, all references to word definition and etymology are taken from the online version of the Oxford English Dictionary (http://dictionary.oed.com), hereafter referred to as the OED.

2. The Nature and Function of Standards

1. While Webster's generally agrees with the OED, Webster's narrative for the definition of standard appears more straightforward.

2. Note the uncritical replication of social value in the notion socio-economic status. The term takes for granted—the ranking of human worth—

what should in fact be explained: the origin of the division of the human group into distinct, ranked categories.

3. Foucault recognized this "pointing" as a means of training, as has Wiggins (1993, chap. 1) in his formulation that all assessments in fact *teach* something.

4. The problem is evident in the discourse on standards, where the words "goal" and "standard" are used interchangeably; a good example can be found with New York State's curriculum. The significance of this point is brought out in the last chapter.

5. A good example of this is the use of different standards for buying and selling during feudal times. Lords, reports Kula (1986, 166), typically had the right to control standards, one for collecting their dues, and another when selling. Such practices would become part of the complaints leveled by all those rebelling against feudal relations that led up to the French Revolution.

3. Academic Achievement and Ability as Forms of Vertical Classification

1. Definitions are from Webster's Unabridged Dictionary. Note as well that they are presented in ranked order (from highest to lowest).

2. For a fuller discussion of the value-laden nature of this terminology, and consistent confusion between facts and values, see Block and Dworkin (1976) and Schiff and Lewontin (1986).

3. "In 1965, the Russell Sage Foundation issued a report entitled 'Experience and Attitudes of American Adults Concerning Standardized Intelligence Tests,'" reports Karier. "The major findings of that report indicated that the effects of these tests on social classes were 'strong and consistent' and that while 'the upper class respondent is more likely to favor the use of tests than the lower class respondent,' the lower class respondent is more likely to see intelligence tests measuring inborn intelligence" (1973, 128).

4. Note that this is not the only kind of political arrangement that emphasizes vertical classification on the basis of mental attributes; as an example, the Chinese civil service exams emerged within a dynastic system.

4. Standardized Tests as Markers of Social Value

1. Note that Gould's well-known *Mismeasure of Man* quotes the first part of this sentence, but leaves out Binet's insistence that he will consider it measurement for "practical reasons" (1981, 151).

2. Debates over whether magnitudes exist prior to measurement, or whether they are the result of measurement, are not uncommon among philosophers of science. Here, I am critical of the one-sidedness of the strictly operational approach that stipulates no quality exists at all, only different kinds of measuring operations exists. Yet naive realism, namely, the view that every quality exists in a given quantity irrespective of the mode and results of measurement, is also suspect as was pointed out in chapter 4. Berka is again helpful here when he argues that "magnitudes are, in substance, of a relational nature. They depend on the procedure of measurement and the resultant numerical values. From this it does not . . . follow that magnitudes do not have an objective basis in reality" (1970, 147–149). Value, on the other hand, is, however, necessarily a product of human social interaction and contingent on historically bound social structures.

3. Ebel and Frisbe make these frank admissions:

> Unlike the inch or pound, the units used in measuring this [scholastic] ability cannot be shown to be equal. The zero point on the ability scale is not clearly defined. Because of these limitations, some of the things we often do [always do, in reality] with test scores, such as finding means and standard deviations, and correlation coefficients, ought not to be done if strict mathematical logic holds sway. Nonetheless, we often find it practically useful to do them. When strict logic conflicts with practical utility, it is the utility that usually wins, as it probably should. (1991, 31)

Suen writes that the "ability of test scores to truthfully reflect quantities of a characteristic of interest actually involves a huge inferential leap" (1990, 5). Steyer begins his work by noting the conclusion of Suppes and Zinnes that "psychological tests are 'pseudopointer instruments,' the readings of which 'do not correspond to any known fundamental or derived numerical assignment'" (Steyer 1989, 26). To provide one more example, Von Broembsen, Gray, and Williams lament the fact that few scientists are willing to undertake theoretical work in measurement. They regrettably admit that there is "no simple correspondence (or isomorphism) between mathematical structures and structures of relations between elements in the social sciences as there are, for example, in mathematical and physical sciences" (1974, 51–52). Yet, in a footnote on the next page, the authors say this problem is given too much attention.

4. Nash elaborates the problems inherent in this approach:

> It is easy to construct a series of questions and treat the resulting form as a scale. Consider, for example, these items, to be rated "agree," "uncertain," "disagree": "I get on well at school." "School is a neat place." "My teachers often praise my work."

So, what do these questions "measure"? This is by no means irrelevant to practice—it is the very question that validity questions are designed to answer. Such items, as anyone with a little knowledge of conventional psychological research will recognize, might easily turn up in a scale designed as an Academic Self-Concept Instrument and they might just as equally turn up on a Pupil School Evaluation Instrument. Furthermore, it is more likely than not that a psychologist employing both "measures" would never so much as look at the test items, but report that the study found Academic Self-Concept . . . to be highly correlated with Pupil School Evaluation and offer that as evidence for the conclusion that pupils with high academic self-concept are also satisfied with their school. (1990, 132)

5. The Rise of Public Education

1. While there is no shortage of literature linking the development of standardized testing with notions of meritocracy, this literature, in my view, undertheorizes the significance of this connection at best (e.g., Karier 1973; Lemann 1999), or give such pronouncements as justifications for an author's view of standardized testing, at worst (e.g., Herrnstein 1973; Sacks 2000). Simple pronouncements that standardized tests are (or are not) measures of merit render as natural the idea that political rights and privileges should be connected to mental characteristics and that reason or intelligence, and therefore schools, should play a key role in the political life of a society and the selection of its leaders. Without a deeper understanding of the significance of this new arrangement emerging out of the struggle against medieval social relations, it is impossible to ascertain the significance of the present drive to eliminate public education "as we know it," and the significance of the role of standards within that movement.

2. Numerous scholars have indicated that the term *feudal* was not used by contemporaries of that time, a finding that has generated some concern about our understanding of political arrangements during the Middle Ages, and the generalizability of that understanding to different parts of Europe, for example (Brown 1974; Reynolds 1994). For purposes here, however, feudalism points in the main to political arrangement accompanying those described by Marx as a mode of agricultural production based on the relation between lords and the peasants who worked their own land and that of the lord. In particular, feudalism involves the exchange of allegiance for a grant of land, typically between two men of noble status.

3. While "aristocracy" originally meant, as with Plato, "rule by the best," by Jefferson's time it had lost this emphasis, hence Jefferson's prefix

"natural" (Lemann 1999, chap. 4). This prefix is not only an attempt to reclaim the original meaning, but reflects the requirement of developing a "natural" means of classification system such that it appears to stand above class, originating outside society. It is an attempt to find a universal standard, immutable and to which all are equally subject, like that of the metric system.

4. On the question of the degree of mobility relative to the introduction of competitive written exams, see Broadfoot's work (1979, chap. 1) and that of Eggleston (1986, chap. 1).

5. To further emphasize the significance of this conception, note that postulating ability as the basis for political rights violates the basic premise of human rights as presented in the Universal Declaration of Human Rights after World War II. In that framework, rights are irrespective of considerations of ability. Human rights exist on the basis of being human and no other consideration whatsoever. They are standards derived from the needs of individuals and collectives of human beings, such that the right to vote for example is premised not on a certain level of education, but simply by virtue of being a member of the body politic. The right to vote and participate in government is justified on the basis that one has a right to participate in that which affects his or her life, not on the basis of having achieved a certain level of education, though the right to education is a claim made in that it is also required to participate in the society.

6. Note that this is a general response to industrialization (see Wilentz 1984), also noted in historical investigations of France in the development of its education system. For example, Harrigan writes, "In an earlier piece, I concluded that the French experience supported Lipset and Bendix's model of those threatened by downward mobility in industrial societies attempting to compensate by encouraging their children to rise through education. After more detailed analysis I now think my interpretation of peasants and shopkeepers fitting such a model incorrect. I preserve my application of it to artisans, whom industrialization directly threatened and whose sons, as we have found, sought new kinds of work" (1980, 146).

7. In this report, Mann presents his argument for the funding of public schools through taxation on the basis that education is a right.

6. Achievement Testing: The Case of Horace Mann

1. Although the word *measured* is used here, it is clear that its content is that of assessment as outlined previously.

2. Examples of these reports are offered in Caldwell and Courtis (1925, 1–9).

3. Several scholars argue that abuses of such a system, where masters only displayed their best students, led to experiments in new forms of examination (e.g., Caldwell and Courtis 1925, 14). However, there is no convincing evidence offered by Smallwood or Kandel—nor is any given by the authors they cite—of such discontent, who was discontent and why. For example Grizzell, who is cited by Kandel, simply states that people were questioning the old methods, yet gives no citation or even anecdotal evidence to articulate this concern (Grizzell 1923, 140). A general review of common schools in Massachusetts by Horace Mann does suggest an overall decline in quality of education, where the upper classes held such schools in contempt (Downs 1974, 31–36).

4. Although historians of education, such as Tyack, are more sensitive to the use of information as a weapon in the battle to reform schools, he too suggests that Mann only succeeded in "provoking a massive rhetorical battle with the masters" (1974, 35) and does not explicitly recognize the role of the information provided by the new exams in expanding state power. While focusing on Philadelphia instead of Boston, Labaree's history of the high school is more explicit about the political use of academic exams by state authorities (1988, 67–73).

5. Given this discussion of the role of efficiency in the rise of standardized testing, some readers may wonder at the absence of a discussion regarding the rise of technocratic rationality, positivism, and scientific management at this juncture or anywhere in the text for that matter. While these ideas are intimately connected to the growth of educational testing during the twentieth century, their role here seems limited. Mann was influenced less by the industrial model, and more by Prussia and China (strong states with limited industrialization). While it may suffice to say that these subjects have already received great attention, a more pointed answer would be that my analysis rests more on psychometry's formal link to American political thought such as opportunity, equality, and fairness, conceptions not readily addressed by critiques of the influence of technocratic thinking on education. Note as well that an emphasis on technocratic thinking as an explanation for the rise of standardized testing implicitly accepts that these tools were adopted for reasons of efficiency.

6. For a general understanding of the leading role the Whig reforms played in antebellum politics, see Howe (1979).

7. Caldwell and Courtis's text contains a reprint of the 1845 *Common School Journal* article in which Mann reprints the committee's report and comments on the results of this new method.

8. One question asks: "On which range of mountains is the line of perpetual snow most elevated above the ocean,—on the Rocky Mountains of North America or on the Cordilleras of Mexico?" Some of the spelling words are as follows: Monotony; Panegyric; Connoisseur; Infatuated.

7. Intelligence Testing: The Case of Alfred Binet

1. See Rutter and his colleagues (1979) for a discussion of the methodological flaws in the original *Coleman Report* and its underestimation of the effects of schooling on students because of its reliance on "ability" tests to measure the impact of instruction.

2. Note that Gould (1981, 151) quotes the first part of this sentence, but leaves out Binet's insistence that he will consider it measurement for practical reasons.

3. For discussion of the difference between measurement, differentiation, and scaling, see Nash (1990). Note that while much is made of "individual differences" in psychology, the use of the word *individual* is often misleading since much of this differentiating is aimed at determining differences among groups of human beings, such that the single human group could be rendered into discrete and qualitatively different categories that were associated with different social roles, rights, and responsibilities.

4. Webster's defines *alienist* as "one that treats diseases of the mind," especially "a physician specializing in legal problems of psychiatry."

5. Note that after the 1905 scale, Binet and Simon use the language of measurement more frequently and rarely use the language of "differential diagnosis."

6. Understanding this approach might help clarify why there are often many possible answers to test questions, not only the one that is deemed correct, or awarded the most points. It is not simply the correctness of the answer, but its quality that is an issue; what constitutes a good answer is necessarily a judgment, from a particular perspective or social position; hence, all those multiple-choice questions, "choose the best answer."

9. The Failure of Testing

1. The part of the NCLB that concretely deals with "national defense"—section 9528 mandates schools turn over student information to military recruiters—has been hushed by government officials, Congress, and major media outlets alike.As this provision of the law becomes known, it becomes a source of outrage and resistance (Molloy 2005).

2. I can no longer use the euphemism "reform" when present efforts are serving to completely destroy the system that came into being in the middle of the nineteenth century. I did this not so much for fidelity to that system but rather in an effort to use accurate language. "Reform" generally connotes improvement, and there is little systematic evidence of anything but the opposite. "Deform," however, connotes a warping and collapsing, which I think is more accurate.

3. I say "as we know it" in response to reformers' efforts to create confusion over what constitutes public education, a notable example being the claim that "charter schools are public schools." If this is so, why the name "charter"? Charter schools and other market-based reforms constitute a radical change in the conception and organization of schooling in the United States.

4. In a March 2004 posting on the Committee on Education and the Workforce Web site entitled "No Child Left Behind: Frequent Questions and Accurate Answers," we are told that "NCLB does not label schools 'failures.' Schools are not punished—they are provided services to help them achieve improved educational performance. If any subgroup in a school does not meet its AYP [adequate yearly progress] goals for two consecutive years, the school is placed in 'school improvement' status (not labeled as 'failures' as some report)" (Miller 2004). Of course, "not meeting expectations" is longhand for "failure" as commonly defined.

5. For those wanting to explore the relevance of human rights for education in general, see, for example, Spring (2001). A useful discussion of rights and opportunities as they relate to education can be found in Esconi and Hurwitz (1974). Also see the Right to Education Project, the only Web site in the world devoted solely to the right to education (http://www.right-to-education.org). It was started by Katarina Tomasevski, the first-ever special rapporteur on the Right to Education of the United Nations Commission on Human Rights, after her appointment in 1998.

References

Airasian, Peter W. 1988. Symbolic validation: The case of state-mandated, high-stakes testing. *Educational Evaluation and Policy Analysis* 10 (4): 301–313.

Apple, Michael W. 2001. *Educating the "right" way: Markets, standards, God, and inequality.* New York: RoutledgeFalmer.

Avanzini, Guy. 1969. *La contribution de Binet a l'elaboration d'une pedagogie scientifique.* Paris: Librairie Philosophique J. Vrin.

Baker, Eva L. 1990. Trends in testing in the USA. *Journal of Education Policy* 5 (5): 139–157.

Behling, C. C. 1980. A history and analysis of educational assessment in the United States. Unpublished dissertation, Education, Wayne State University, Detroit.

Berka, Karel. 1970. Methodological problems of measurement. *Problems of the Science of Science* 1:143–153.

Berka, Karel. 1983. *Measurement: Its concepts, theories, and problems,* trans. A. Riska. Boston Studies in the Philosophy of Science, vol. 72. Boston: Kluwer.

Berliner, David C. 1993. Educational reform in an era of disinformation. *Education Policy Analysis Archives* 1 (2). Available at http://epaa.asu.edu/epaa/v1n2.html.

Bernstein, Dennis. 2001. *A coup against the American constitution: An interview with professor Francis A. Boyle.* rat haus reality press [April 10, 2003]. Available at http://www.ratical.org/ratville/CAH/fab111401.html.

Binet, Alfred, and Théodore Simon. 1916. *The development of intelligence in children (the Binet-Simon scale),* trans. E. S. Kite. Vineland: Training School at Vineland, New Jersey, Department of Research.

Binet, Alfred, and Théodore Simon. 1922. *Les enfants anormaux,* 4th ed. Paris: Librairie Armand Colin.

Block, N. J., and Gerald Dworkin. 1976. IQ, heritability, and inequality. In *The IQ Controversy,* ed. N. J. Block and G. Dworkin. New York: Pantheon.

Bonnell, Victoria E. 1980. The uses of theory, concepts, and comparison in historical sociology. *Comparative Studies in Society and History* 22:156–175.

Bracey, Gerald W. 1995. *Final exam: A study of the perpetual scrutiny of American education—Historical perspectives on assessment, standards, outcomes, and criticism of U.S. public schools,* 1st ed. Bloomington, IN: Technos Press.

123

Bracey, Gerald W. 1999. The propaganda of "a nation at risk." Education Disinformation Detection and Reporting Agency. Available at http://www.america-tomorrow.com/bracey/EDDRA/EDDRA8.htm.

Bracey, Gerald. 2002. *The war against America's public schools: Privatizing schools, commercializing education.* Boston: Allyn and Bacon.

Bracey, Gerald. 2003. *On the death of child and the destruction of public schools.* Portsmouth, NH: Heinemann.

Broadfoot, Patricia. 1979. *Assessment, schools and society,* ed. J. Eggleston. Contemporary Sociology of the School Series. London: Methuen.

Broadfoot, Patricia. 1996. *Education, assessment and society,* ed. H. Torrance. Assessing Assessment Series. Buckingham, UK: The Open University.

Brown, E. A. R. 1974. The tyranny of a construct: Feudalism and the historians of medieval Europe. *American Historical Review* 79 (2): 1063–1088.

Business Roundtable. 1998, November. Building support for tests that count. Available at http://www.brtable.org/pdf/225.pdf.

Caldwell, Ottis W., and Stuart A. Courtis. 1925. *Then and now in education: 1645–1923.* New York: World Book.

Calhoun, Craig J. 1992. *Habermas and the public sphere.* Studies in Contemporary German Social Thought. Cambridge: MIT Press.

Carson, John S. 1994. *Talents, intelligence and the construction of human difference in France and America, 1760–1920.* Unpublished dissertation, Department of History, Princeton University, Princeton, NJ.

Chapman, Paul D. 1988. *Schools as sorters: Lewis M. Terman, applied psychology and the intelligence testing movement, 1890–1930.* New York: New York University Press.

Cicourel, Aaron V. 1964. *Method and measurement in sociology.* London: Free Press.

Coleman, James. 1977. The concept of equality of educational opportunity. In *School and society: A sociological reader,* ed. B. R. Cosin, I. R. Dale, G. M. Esland, D. MacKinnon, and D. F. Swift. London: Routledge and Kegan Paul, in association with The Open University Press.

Conley, David T. 2003. *Who governs our schools? Changing roles and responsibilities.* New York: Teachers College Press.

Cremin, Lawrence A., ed. 1957. *The republic and the school: Horace Mann on the education of free men.* New York: Teachers College, Columbia University.

Dahrendorf, Ralf. 1968. *Essays in the theory of society.* Stanford, CA: Stanford University Press.

Dorn, Sherman. 1998. The political legacy of school accountability systems. *Education Policy Analysis Archives* 6 (1). Available at http://olam.ed.asu.edu/epaa/v6n1.

Dorn, Sherman. 2007. *Accountability Frankenstein: Understanding and taming the monster.* Charlotte, NC: Information Age Publishing.

Downs, Robert B. 1974. *Horace Mann: Champion of public schools.* New York: Twayne.

DuBois, Philip H. 1970. *A history of psychological testing.* Boston: Allyn and Bacon.

Durkheim, Emile. 1977. *The evolution of educational thought: Lectures on the formation and development of secondary education in France.* London: Routledge and Kegan Paul.

Ebel, Robert L. 1972. *Essentials of educational measurement*. Englewood Cliffs, NJ: Prentice Hall.

Ebel, Robert L., and David A. Frisbie. 1991. *Essentials of educational measurement*. Englewood Cliffs, NJ: Prentice Hall.

Education Commission of the States. 1999. *The changing landscape of education governance*. Denver, CO: Author.

Eggleston, John. 1986. Examining school examinations: A sociological commentary. *New Education* 8 (1): 59–69.

Epstein, Jane E. 1998. *Power, politics and the National Assessment of Educational Progress*. Unpublished dissertation, Education, Wayne State University, Detroit.

Esconi, Charles A., and Emauel. Hurwitz, eds. 1974. *Education for whom? The question of equal educational opportunity*. New York: Dodd, Mead.

Fairfield, Roy P., ed. 1961. *The Federalist Papers: A collection of essays written in support of the Constitution of the United States, from the original text of Alexander Hamilton, James Madison, John Jay*. Garden City, NY: Anchor Books.

Finn, Chester E. 2004. Lost at sea. *Education Next* (Summer): 16–18.

Fuller, Bruce, Joseph Wright, Kathryn Gesicki, and Erin Kang. 2007. Gauging growth: How to judge No Child Left Behind? *Educational Researcher 36* (5): 268–278.

Gardner, Howard. 1993. *Frames of mind: The theory of multiple intelligences*, 2d ed. New York: Basic Books.

Gentile, J. Ronald. 1997. *Educational psychology*, 2d ed. Dubuque, IA: Kendall/Hunt.

Gifford, Bernard R. 1986. Epilogue: Testing, politics, and the allocation of opportunities. *Journal of Negro Education 55* (3): 422–436.

Giroux, Henry A. 2004. *The terror of neoliberalism*. Boulder, CO: Paradigm.

Glenn, Charles L. 1988. *The myth of the common school*. Amherst: University of Massachusetts Press.

Gould, Stephen J. 1981. *The mismeasure of man*. New York: Norton.

Green, Andy. 1990. *Education and state formation: The rise of education systems in England, France, and the USA*. New York: St. Martin's Press.

Grizzell, Emit D. 1923. *Origin and development of the high school in New England before 1865*. New York: Macmillan.

Handel, Michael J. 2003. Skills mismatch in the labor market. *American Review of Sociology* 29:135–165.

Haney, Walter. 1977. The measurement of educational equality. Unpublished dissertation, Graduate School of Education, Harvard University, Boston.

Haney, Walter. 1984. Testing reasoning and reasoning about testing. *Review of Educational Research 54* (4): 597–654.

Haney, Walter. 2000. The myth of the Texas miracle in education. *Education Policy Analysis Archives* 8 (41). Available at http://epaa.asu.edu/epaa/v8n41/.

Haney, Walter, and George Madaus. 1989. Searching for alternative to standardized tests: Whys, whats, and whithers. *Phi Delta Kappan* 70 (9): 683–687.

Haney, Walter, George F. Madaus, and Robert Lyons. 1993. *The fractured marketplace for standardized testing*. Boston: Kluwer.

Hanson, F. Allan. 1993. *Testing testing: Social consequences of the examined life.* Berkeley and Los Angeles: University of California Press.

Harrigan, Patrick J. 1980. *Mobility, elites, and education in French society of the second empire.* Waterloo, ON: Wilfrid Laurier University Press.

Herrnstein, R. J. 1973. *I.Q. In the meritocracy.* Boston: Little, Brown.

Hess, Frederick M. 2002. *Making sense of the "public" in public education.* Washington, DC: Progressive Policy Institute.

Hlebowitsh, Peter S. 1990. Playing power politics: How "A Nation at Risk" achieved its national stature. *Journal of Research and Development in Education* 23 (2): 82–88.

Hobbes, Thomas. 1909. *Hobbes's leviathan: Reprinted from edition of 1651.* Oxford, UK: Clarendon Press.

Hopkins, K. D., J. C. Stanley, and B. R. Hopkins. 1990. *Educational and psychological measurement and evaluation.* Englewood Cliffs, NJ: Prentice Hall.

Hoskin, Keith. 1979. The examination, disciplinary power and rational schooling. *History of Education* 8 (2): 135–147.

Howe, Daniel Walker. 1979. *The political culture of the American Whigs.* Chicago: University of Chicago Press.

Jefferson, Thomas. 1813. The Natural Aristocracy. Available at http://www.tncrimlaw.com/civil_bible/natural_aristocracy.htm.

Jefferson, Thomas. 1971. Letter to Joseph Cabell, 1818. In *American writings on popular education: The nineteenth century,* ed. R. Welter. Indianapolis, IN: Bobbs-Merrill.

Johnson, Chalmers. 2007. *Nemesis: The last days of the American republic.* New York: Metropolitan Books.

Kaestle, Carl F. 1983. *Pillars of the republic: Common schools and American society, 1780-1860,* 1st ed. New York: Hill and Wang.

Kamin, Loen J. 1974. *The science and politics of I.Q.* New York: Wiley.

Kandel, Isaac Leon. 1936. *Examinations and their substitutes in the United States.* New York: Carnegie Foundation for the Advancement of Teaching.

Karier, Clarence. 1973. Testing for order and control in the corporate liberal state. In *Roots of crisis: American education in the twentieth century,* ed. C. Karier, P. C. Violas, and J. Spring. Chicago: Rand McNally.

Katz, Michael B. 1968. *The irony of early school reform: Educational innovation in mid-nineteenth century Massachusetts.* Cambridge: Harvard University Press.

Katznelson, Ira, and Margaret Weir. 1985. *Schooling for all.* New York: Basic Books.

Kellaghan, Thomas, George F. Madaus, and Peter W. Airasian. 1982. *The effects of standardized testing.* Boston: Kluwer-Hijhoff.

Kliebard, Herbert M. 1986. *The struggle for the American curriculum, 1893-1958.* Boston: Routledge and Kegan Paul.

Kracke, E. A. 1963. Region, family, and individual in the examination system. In *The Chinese civil service: Career open to talent?* ed. J. M. Menzel. Boston: Heath.

Krone, Emily. 2008. Dist. 93 against giving tests to kids still learning English. *Daily Herald*, February 22.

Kula, Witold. 1986. *Measures and men*. Princeton, NJ: Princeton University Press.

Labaree, David F. 1988. *The making of an American high school: The credentials market and the central high school of Philadelphia, 1838–1939*. New Haven, CT: Yale University Press.

Lemann, Nicholas. 1999. *The big test*. New York: Farrar, Straus and Giroux.

Linn, Robert. 2000. Assessment and accountability. *Educational Researcher* 29 (2): 4–16.

Lipman, Pauline. 2002. Making the global city, making inequality: The political economy and cultural politics of Chicago school policy. *American Educational Research Journal* 39 (2): 379–419.

Lorge, Irving. [1951] 1996. The fundamental nature of measurement. In *Educational measurement: Origins, theories and explications*, ed. A. W. Ward, H. W. Stoker, and M. M. Ward. New York: University Press of America.

Madaus, G. F. 1990. *Testing as a social technology*. Boston: Boston College.

Madaus, George F., and Laura M. O'Dwyer. 1999. A short history of performance assessment. *Phi Delta Kappan* (May): 688–695.

Mann, Horace. 1847. *Tenth annual report concerning the year 1846*. Facsimile ed. Boston: Dutton and Wentworth, State Printers.

Mann, Horace. [1855] 1969. *Lectures on education*. New York: Arno Press and The New York Times.

Mann, Horace. 1868. *Life and Works of Horace Mann*, ed. M. Mann, vol. 3. Boston: Horace B. Fuller.

Mann, Horace. 1965. *Horace Mann on the crisis in education*, ed. L. Filler. Yellow Springs, OH: Antioch Press.

Mathews, J. C. 1985. *Examinations: A commentary*. London: George Allen and Urwin.

Mathison, Sandra, and E. Wayne Ross. 2002. The hegemony of accountability in schools and universities. *Workplace: The Journal of Academic Labor* 5 (1). Available at http://www.louisville.edu/journal/workplace/issue5p1/mathison.html.

McDonnell, Lorraine M. 2004. *Politics, persuasion, and educational testing*. Cambridge: Harvard University Press.

McNeil, Linda M. 2000. *Contradictions of school reform: Educational costs of standardized testing*. New York: Routledge.

McNeil, Linda M., Eileen Coppola, Judy Radigan, and Julian Vasquez Heilig. 2008. Avoidable losses: High-stakes accountability and the dropout crisis. *Education Policy Analysis Archives* 16 (3). Retrieved February 1, 2008. Available at http://epaa.asu.edu/epaa/v16n3/.

Meier, Deborah, ed. 2000. *Will standards save public education?* Boston: Beacon Press.

Mensh, Elaine, and Harry Mensh. 1991. *The IQ mythology: Class, race, gender, and inequality*. Carbondale: Southern Illinois University Press.

Menzel, Johanna Margarete, ed. 1963. *The Chinese civil service: Career open to talent? Problems in Asian civilizations*. Boston: Heath.

Miller, George. 2004, March 9. No child left behind: Frequent questions and accurate answers: Committee on Education and the Workforce. Available at http://edworkforce.house.gov/democrats/eseainfo.html.

Milofsky, Carl. 1989. *Testers and testing: The sociology of school psychology.* New Brunswick, NJ: Rutgers University Press.

Molloy, Aimee. 2005. No child left unrecruited. *Salon.com*, March 21.

Montgomery, Robert J. 1967. *Examinations: An account of their evolution as administrative devices in England*, ed. W. H. E. Johnson. Studies in Comparative Education. Pittsburgh: University of Pittsburgh.

Montgomery, Robert J. 1978. *A new examination of examinations.* London: Routledge and Kegan Paul.

Mulhern, James. 1933. *A history of secondary education in Pennsylvania.* Philadelphia: Author.

Nash, Roy. 1990. *Intelligence and realism: A materialist critique of IQ.* New York: St. Martin's Press.

National Commission on Excellence in Education. 1983. *A nation at risk: The imperative for educational reform.* Washington, DC: Author.

National Commission on Testing and Public Policy. 1990. *From gatekeeper to gateway: Transforming testing in America.* Chestnut Hill, MA: Author.

National Education Association. 2005. NCLB testing results offer "complex, muddled" picture. *Issues in Education.* Available at http://www.nea.org/esea/ayptrends1104.html.

National Education Association. 2006. More schools are failing NCLB law's "adequate yearly progress" requirements. *Issues in Education.* Available at http://www.nea.org/esea/ayptrends0106.html.

Nichols, Sharon Lynn, and David C. Berliner. 2007. *Collateral damage: How high-stakes testing corrupts America's schools.* Cambridge: Harvard Education Press.

Noddings, Nel. 1997. Thinking about standards. *Phi Delta Kappan* 79 (3): 184–189.

Office of Technology Assessment. 1992. *Testing in American schools: Asking the right questions.* Washington, DC: U.S. Congress.

Orfield, Gary, and Mindy L Kornhaber. 2001. *Raising standards or raising barriers? Inequality and high-stakes testing in public education.* New York: Century Foundation Press.

Pawson, Roy. 1986. On the level: Measurement scales and sociological theory. *Bulletin de M'ethodologie Sociologique* 11 (July): 49-82.

Pawson, Ray. 1989. *A measure for measures: A manifesto for empirical sociology.* London: Routledge.

Pile, Emily. 2005. Te$t market: High-stakes tests aren't good for students, teachers, or schools. So who are they good for? *Texas Observer*, May 13.

Popham, James. 1999. Why standardized tests don't measure educational quality. *Educational Leadership* 56 (6): 8–15.

Ravitch, Diane, and Joseph P. Viteritti. 1997. *New schools for a new century: The redesign of urban education.* New Haven, CT: Yale University Press.

Reese, William J. 1995. *The origins of the American high school.* New Haven, CT: Yale University Press.

Reese, William J. 2007. *History, education, and the schools.* New York: Palgrave Macmillan.

Resnick, Daniel P. 1981. Testing in America: A supportive environment. *Phi Delta Kappan* 62 (9): 625–628.

Resnick, Daniel P. 1982. History of educational testing. In *Ability testing: Uses, consequences, controversies, part 2: Documentation section,* ed. A. K. Wigdor and W. R. Garner. Washington DC: National Academy Press.

Reynolds, Susan. 1994. *Fiefs and vassals: The medieval evidence reinterpreted.* Oxford, UK: Oxford University Press.

Ringer, Fritz. 1987. On segmentation in modern European education systems: The case of French secondary education, 1865-1920. In *The rise of the modern educational system: Structural change and social reproduction, 1870-1920,* ed. D. K. Muller, F. Ringer, and B. Simon. Cambridge, MA: Cambridge University Press.

Roach, John. 1971. *Public examinations in England 1850–1900,* ed. A. C. F. Beales, A. V. Judges, and J. P. C. Roach. Cambridge Texts and Studies in the History of Education. London: Cambridge University Press.

Rothstein, Richard. 2007. Leaving "No Child Left Behind" behind. *American Prospect,* December 17.

Ruch, Giles Murrel. 1929. *The objective or new-type examination: An introduction to educational measurement.* Chicago: Scott, Foresman.

Rutter, Michael, Barbara Maughan, Peter Mortimore, Janet Ouston, and Alan Smith. 1979. *Fifteen thousand hours: Secondary schools and their effects on children.* Cambridge: Harvard University Press.

Sacks, Peter. 2000. *Standardized minds: The high price of America's testing culture and what we can do to change it.* Cambridge, MA: Perseus Books.

Saltman, Kenneth J. 2000. *Collateral damage: Corporatizing public schools— A threat to democracy.* Lanham, MD: Rowman and Littlefield.

Saltman, Kenneth J. 2005. *The Edison schools: Corporate schooling and the assault on public education.* New York: Routledge.

Sarason, Seymour B. 1976. The unfortunate fate of Alfred Binet and school psychology. *Teachers College Record* 77 (4): 579–592.

Schiff, Michel, and Richard Lewontin. 1986. *Education and class: The irrelevance of IQ genetic studies.* Oxford, UK: Clarendon Press.

Schultz, Stanley K. 1973. *The culture factory: Boston public schools, 1789–1860.* New York: Oxford University Press.

Shaker, Erika. 1998. *The North American education industry and education restructuring in Canada.* Ottawa, ON: Canadian Center for Policy Alternatives.

Smallwood, Mary Lovett. 1935. *An historical study of examinations and grading systems in early American universities.* Cambridge: Harvard University Press.

Smith, Mary Lee. 1996. *The politics of assessment: A view from the political culture of Arizona.* Los Angeles: National Center for Research on Evaluation, Standards, and Student Testing (CRESST).

Smith, Mary Lee, Walter Heinecke, and Audrey Noble. 1999. Assessment policy and political spectacle. *Teachers College Record* 101 (2): 157–191.

Spring, Joel. 2001. *Globalization and educational rights: An intercivilizational analysis*. Mahwah, NJ: Erlbaum.

Stedman, Lawrence C. 1996. Respecting the evidence: The achievement crisis remains real. *Education Policy Analysis Archives* 4 (7). Available at http://epaa.asu.edu/epaa/v4n7.html.

Steyer, Rolf. 1989. Models of classical psychometric test theory as stochastic measurement models: Representation, uniqueness, meaningfulness, identifiability and testability. *Methodika* 3: 25–60.

Stock-Morton, Phyllis. 1988. *Moral education for a secular society: The development of morale laïque in nineteenth-century France*. Albany: State University of New York Press.

Suen, Hoi K. 1990. *Principles of test theories*. Hillsdale, NJ: Erlbaum.

Suskind, Ron. 2004. Without a doubt. *New York Times Magazine,* October 17.

Tilly, Charles. 1981. *As sociology meets history*. New York: Academic Press.

Trow, Martin. 1996. Trust, markets and accountability in higher education: A comparative perspective. *Higher Education Policy* 9 (4): 309–324.

Tuddenham, Read D. 1962. The nature and measurement of intelligence. In *Psychology in the making*, ed. L. Postman. New York: Knopf.

Tyack, David B. 1974. *The one best system*. Cambridge: Harvard University Press.

Tyack, David B., Thomas James, and Aaron Benavot. 1987. *Law and the shaping of public education, 1785-1954*. Madison: University of Wisconsin Press.

Von Broembsen, Maximilian H., Louis N. Gray, and J, Sherwood Williams. 1974. Formalization and verification of theory in the behavioral sciences. *International Behavioral Scientist* 6 (4): 51–67.

Walsh, Mark. 2008. Court revives NEA suit against NCLB. *Education Week,* January 8.

Weber, Eugen. 1976. *Peasants into Frenchmen*. Stanford, CA: Stanford University Press.

Welter, Rush. 1962. *Popular education and democratic thought in America*. New York: Columbia University Press.

Welter, Rush, ed. 1971. *American writings on popular education: The nineteenth century*. Indianapolis: Bobbs-Merrill.

Wesson, Kenneth. 2000. The "Volvo effect." *Education Week,* November 22.

Wiggins, Grant. 1991. Standards, not standardization: Evoking quality student work. *Educational Leadership* 48 (5): 18–25.

Wiggins, Grant. 1993. *Assessing student performance*. San Francisco: Jossey-Bass.

Wilentz, Sean. 1984. *Chants democratic: New York City and the rise of the American working class, 1788-1850*. New York: Oxford University Press.

Williams, Richard. 1990. *Hierarchical structures and social value: The creation of black and Irish identities in the United States*. Cambridge: Cambridge University Press.

Wilson, Noel. 1998. Educational standards and the problem of error. *Educational Policy Analysis Archives* 6 (10). Available at http://epaa.asu.edu/epaa/v6n10/.

Wilson, Thomas A. 1996. *Reaching for a better standard: English school inspection and the dilemma of accountability for American schools*. New York: Teachers College.

Woestehoff, Julie, and Monty Neill. 2007. Chicago school reform: Lessons for the nation. Cambridge, MA: National Center for Fair and Open Testing (FairTest) and Parents United for Responsible Education (PURE).

Wolf, Theta H. 1973. *Alfred Binet.* Chicago: University of Chicago Press.

Wooten, Kenneth L. 1982. Tests: The foundation for equality. *New Directions for Testing and Measurement* 16:11-16.

Yerkes, Robert. 1987. The mental rating of school children. In *Justice, ideology, and education*, ed. Edward Stevens Jr. and G. H. Wood. New York: McGraw Hill.

Index